VISUO-SPATIAL WORKING MEMORY AND INDIVIDUAL DIFFERENCES

Essays in Cognitive Psychology
UK Editors:
Alan Baddeley, *University of Bristol, UK*
Vicki Bruce, *University of Stirling, UK*

North American Editor:
Henry L. Roediger, III, *Washington University in St. Louis, USA*

Essays in Cognitive Psychology is designed to meet the need for rapid publication of brief volumes in cognitive psychology. Primary topics will include perception, movement and action, attention, memory, mental representation, language, and problem solving. Furthermore, the series seeks to define cognitive psychology in its broadest sense, encompassing all topics either informed by, or informing, the study of mental processes. As such, it covers a wide range of subjects including computational approaches to cognition, cognitive neuroscience, social cognition, and cognitive development, as well as areas more traditionally defined as cognitive psychology. Each volume in the series will make a conceptual contribution to the topic by reviewing and synthesizing the existing research literature, by advancing theory in the area, or by some combination of these missions. The principal aim is that authors will provide an overview of their own highly successful research program in an area. It is also expected that volumes will, to some extent, include an assessment of current knowledge and identification of possible future trends in research. Each book will be a self-contained unit supplying the advanced reader with a well-structured review of the work described and evaluated.

Also available in this series:

Visuo-Spatial Working Memory and Individual Differences

Cesare Cornoldi

Professor of Psychology, University of Padua, Italy

Tomaso Vecchi

Professor of Psychology, University of Pavia, Italy

 **Psychology Press**
Taylor & Francis Group

HOVE AND NEW YORK

First published 2003
by Psychology Press
27 Church Road, Hove, East Sussex, BN3 2FA

Simultaneously published in the USA and Canada
by Psychology Press
29 West 35th Street, New York, NY 10001

Psychology Press is a member of the Taylor & Francis Group

Copyright © 2003 Psychology Press

Typeset in Times by RefineCatch Limited, Bungay, Suffolk
Printed and bound in Great Britain by
TJ International Ltd, Padstow, Cornwall

Cover design by Bob Rowinski at Code 5 Design

British Library Cataloguing in Publication Data
A catalogue record for this book is available from the British Library

Library of Congress Cataloging-in-Publication Data

Cornoldi, Cesare.
Visuo-spatial working memory and individual differences / Cesare
Cornoldi & Tomaso Vecchi.
p. cm. – (Essays in cognitive psychology)
Includes bibliographical references and index.
ISBN 1–84169–216–6 (alk. paper)
1. Short-term memory. 2. Space perception. 3. Visual perception.
4. Individual differences. I. Vecchi, Tomaso, 1966– II. Title. III.
Series.
BF378.S54 C67 2003
153.1′32 – dc21
2002012455

ISBN 1-84169-216-6

Contents

Preface

The concept of working memory has acquired a crucial role within cognitive psychology. Its importance resides in the fact that the human mind cannot operate without the support of a temporary memory system, holding and processing information to carry out cognitive tasks. Successes and failures in many activities could then be due to, respectively, an efficient or weak functioning of working memory. In this volume we have examined the specific characteristics of the visuo-spatial component of working memory, assumed to be critical in a variety of human activities like perception, action, imagery, or orientation. Our effort was directed towards two main goals. The first goal was to explore the organization and features of visuo-spatial working memory within the more general framework of the working memory system. The second goal was to examine the implications of visuo-spatial working memory limitations in the study of specific populations who, for different reasons, are differentially affected by them. These two goals are strictly interconnected, justifying our approach to the study of working memory from an individual differences perspective. To this aim, we then integrated empirical data, mostly deriving from our own studies, in order to provide an updated overview of this field of research.

Acknowledgements

We are indebted to many friends and colleagues who helped and reinforced us in many ways during the period on which the research reported in this book is spanned. In particular, Rossana De Beni, Luisa Girelli, Paola Palladino, and Francesca Pazzaglia generously gave scientific advice and personal support. Many students offered gentle and hard questions and we are much indebted to them for their collaboration as well as for improving our ideas. A special "thank you" to Nicola Mammarella who provided thoughtful and constant help. Diego Varotto, Francesco Nigito, and Maria Luisa Tritto offered technical and human support: The figures and tables are due to them. Caroline Clark transformed our manuscript into a more clearly written book.

Over the last 10 years, we have worked in several departments and universities—Padova, Milano, Brunel, Aberdeen, Roma, Pavia—and we always found a friendly and stimulating atmosphere. We would like to take this opportunity to thank all the people who participated in our experiments: Their benevolence allowed us to undertake scientific research in often difficult contexts. Bob Logie and John Richardson carefully read the original manuscript and improved our work through comments and suggestions. Over the years, we received financial support from the National Research Council, the Italian Ministry for University and Scientific Research, the European Union, and the Wellcome Trust.

Introduction

The number of studies investigating visuo-spatial representation, mental imagery, and visuo-spatial cognition in general, has increased greatly in the last 20 years. This growing interest is due to the importance of understanding the specific mechanisms underlying visuo-spatial cognition and the relationship between this area of research and more general issues in cognitive psychology, such as visual perception, action, working memory, central/executive processes, and theoretical models of memory functions (for a review see Denis, Logie, Cornoldi, De Vega, & Engelkamp, 2001a).

Rapid growth in this field of research has produced a variety of theoretical approaches, and has also led to some difficulty adopting a homogeneous set of definitions to describe the boundaries of the area, suggesting a relationship between related fields. For example, the relationship between mental imagery, high-level perception, spatial cognition, and visuo-spatial working memory is rather unclear and researchers give different meaning to the various terms. The nonhomogeneous use of definitions reflects, at least in part, differences in the theoretical positions adopted to account for mental imagery processes, such as the one proposed by Kosslyn (1994) or the perspective adopted by memory theorists, such as Baddeley (1986) or Logie (1995). Specific frames of reference, as well as methodologies, can often be used as keys to interpret different authors' positions.

Fields that appear to be closely related in recent theoretical accounts, such as spatial cognition and mental imagery, have developed from very different historical traditions. Spatial competence has often been linked to the

1

development of the human mind and the capacity necessary for finding one's way around the environment. In these terms, every animal has developed capacities that can be grouped as "intuitive geometries" (Wynn, 1989), that is, spatial competence learnt in everyday life through personal experience. The relationship between spatial competence and motor components is thus very close. It is assumed that spatial competence developed phylogenetically to support movement and motor navigation. Basic spatial abilities have nothing in common with earlier accounts of mental imagery, mainly defined as a form of visual memory. This interpretation was adopted by early theorists of memory ability in the Middle Ages, with the "discovery" of visual images as tools to enhance memory ability. Even Galton, in 1883, defined mental imagery only in terms of visual characteristics such as illumination, definition, and colour. At the end of the nineteenth century, investigation into mental imagery was dedicated simply to defining the variables that could make a mental image more or less vivid, although it was also evident that a mental image is much more complex a phenomenon than the simple reproduction of a scene or picture in terms of its visual characteristics.

In this introductory chapter we will provide a brief summary of definitions and frameworks that have been used to investigate spatial cognition, mental imagery, and their relationship with cognitive models of memory, working memory in particular. Finally, we will propose that spatial and imagery processes can all be viewed as part of a more general visuo-spatial system, requiring the temporary storage and processing of information, and hence linked to working memory activity.

SPATIAL COGNITION

Spatial cognition has many different facets and has been considered in various ways. For example, spatial competence is typically associated with comprehending geometric properties such as distance and size, as well as physical properties such as velocity and mass (the idea of an intuitive geometry is closely linked to an intuitive physics; Eilan, 1993). These concepts may give us a view of the phylogenetic development of spatial abilities in humans and also the ontogenesis of their development in children. Nevertheless, they provide only a scarce definition of what can be called "spatial processes." The problem of defining the concept of "spatial" is not new and reflects the variety of different approaches that have been used to investigate spatial cognition.

The notion of spatial skills is very often related to a person's ability to move in space and navigate in the environment. This ability is of paramount importance in everyday activities and it is not surprising that spatial skills are often confused with navigational ability. As underlined above, the evolution of spatial competence has been linked to motor functions; thus the ability to move and find one's way in the environment clearly requires an understanding of the spatial properties of that environment. It is possible to encode spatial information in an egocentric or allocentric representation (Foreman & Gillet, 1997). An egocentric spatial representation refers to spatial encoding of information as a function of body position or a self-centred system of spatial coordinates. On the other hand, an allocentric spatial representation is based on the relationship between two or more objects in space. This relationship is defined not by means of the body's orientation or distance, but in terms of their spatial relations. It is clear that both egocentric and allocentric spatial representations are linked to motor functions, either in terms of grasping and reaching abilities (egocentric representations) or in terms of body movement and navigational ability (egocentric or allocentric representations).

A close link between spatial and motor functions has often been suggested and several investigations have given empirical support to this idea. Arm movements have been shown to specifically impair maintenance of spatially based representations (see Johnson, 1982; Smyth, Pearson, & Pendleton, 1988). It can be suggested that body movement automatically determines the generation of a specific spatial representation that is used to continuously monitor position in space. A close relationship between visuo-spatial representations and motor ability has also been suggested by Milner and Goodale (1995) in a theoretical model of visuo-spatial functions comprising two different systems. A visuo-motor system is involved in encoding and processing visual information used to plan movement. An alternative structure processes spatial information necessary for generating more complex mental images and spatial representations.

These ideas are related to the distinction between visual and spatial processes, which has its roots in studies carried out in the field of psychology of perception. These ideas were developed by Ungerleider and Mishkin (1982) who showed the importance of differentiating between a "what" system (for recognising the specific features of a perceived object) and a "where" system (for locating that object in space) within the visual cortex. These studies were carried out while investigating perceptual functions in animals but led to research in human cognitive experimental psychology and neuropsychology. With reference to higher imagery functions, several studies have differentiated between visual and spatial processes in mental representations (Farah, Hammond, Levine, & Calvanio, 1988; Logie & Marchetti, 1991). These studies succeeded in dissociating the processing of visual (such as colour, shape, and texture) from spatial characteristics (such as relative or absolute distance, positions, and metrical relations) in mental representations. These data highlight the need for a closer analysis of the specific characteristics of information to be processed.

In terms of everyday activities and spatial orientation, the distinction between what/visual and where/spatial processes has also been conceptualised in terms of the ability to recognise places and landmarks as opposed to the ability to encode spatial relationships in orientation tasks (Pazzaglia & Cornoldi, 1999). Studies of patients selectively impaired in either ability confirm that the two deficits can be considered separately within topographical disorientation (topographical agnosia and topographical amnesia; see De Renzi, 1982). A number of other studies are reviewed in Chapters 1 and 2, suggesting that many other dissociations may be proposed within the spatial dimension.

These data offer an interesting, but unfortunately somewhat unclear, pattern and raise doubts about what can be called "spatial." What is the relationship between perception and internal spatial representations? Superficially, the development of spatial skills as a function of intuitive geometrical or physical relations seems to indicate the interdependence of perception and spatial representation. However, on closer analysis, although the original stimuli come from visual perception, it seems that mental processes engaged in generating spatial representations do not necessarily depend on visual perception. This point is associated with the debate concerning mental imagery.

VISUAL MENTAL IMAGERY

One of the main issues in the study of visuo-spatial cognition concerns mental visuo-spatial representations that assume the form of mental images. As reported above, in the past, visual mental imagery was often considered as the capacity to build an internal picture of an object or scene, and its characteristics were defined in terms of vividness and perception-like features (see Cornoldi, De Beni, Giusberti, Marucci, Massironi, & Mazzoni, 1991a). The assumption that mental imagery is a surrogate of visual perception is therefore not new, and is still shared by some researchers. From an introspective point of view, this is clearly the way the imagery problem should be addressed. For example, we all have a subjective sensation that a mental representation should be as similar to visual perception as possible. This sensation has been considered a source of artefact (Pylyshyn, 1973) or modification while reflecting on the functional properties of mental images.

Over the last 30 years, starting with the pioneering contribution of Shepard and Metzler (1971), the study of mental imagery has moved towards the consideration of spatial processes. Kosslyn (1980, 1994) developed a very coherent model of imagery processes based on the characteristics that can be found in perceptual processing. Kosslyn's theory has its roots in the assumption that imagery processes overlap substantially with perceptual processes and, therefore, a detailed account of high-level vision should also provide a sound model of mental imagery. A typical account of studies reporting perception and imagery as equivalent can be found in data obtained using the mental scanning technique. The first study confirming the equivalence between perceptual and imagery processes using this technique was reported by Kosslyn (1973), who found that scanning time was dependent on relative distance not only in visual perception but also in mental imagery. That is, the time needed to transfer the focus from one part of the external world to another was due to the relative distance between those parts.

However, mental imagery cannot be identified with visual perception. Other processes could be involved and, specifically, a relationship between long-term associative memory should be postulated. For example, Kosslyn (1994) suggests that mental imagery is linked with the object-recognition process. This process is interpreted to define high-level vision, that is, an interaction between perceptual processes and long-term knowledge in a vision-like system. As a consequence, the object-recognition process provides a useful analogy with the process of imagery generation. Kosslyn (1994) described very specifically the various components and subsystems that should be hypothesised in an object-recognition system and, similarly, in an imagery model.

Other theories of mental imagery (e.g., Cornoldi, De Beni, Giusberti, & Massironi, 1998) have suggested that the distance between visual perception and visuo-spatial mental imagery may be greater than assumed in the past, especially in the case of mental images not directly derived from visual experience. In fact, visuo-spatial mental imagery does not necessarily originate from information sharing the same visuo-spatial format. Imagery can be defined as a mental process with output in an internal visuo-spatial representation. It is important to underline that visuo-spatial representations may originate from a variety of perceptual stimuli (not only visual but also haptic or verbal information) as well as from information stored in long-term memory, without the need for an external associative aid to recall the appropriate information.

In particular, there is strong empirical evidence regarding the congenitally nonsighted (see Chapter 6), showing that mental images can be generated in the total absence of visual perception. Data obtained with nonsighted subjects show that visual input is not a necessary condition for generating mental images with the same functional properties that visuo-spatial mental images have for sighted people. Within this framework, the relationship between perceptual and imagery systems needs to be clarified. On the one hand, it is possible that the existence of equivalent processes in perception and imagery is due to the use of common structures; on the other, different structures could have developed in a functionally similar manner due to similarities in the information to be processed.

WORKING MEMORY

The concept of working memory (WM) was initially proposed by Baddeley and Hitch (1974) and developed by Baddeley (1986), and is characterised by the assumption that short-term storage of information must be considered as part of a more complex system involved in the execution of a specific task. The information is stored in the WM as long as necessary, and the structure need not be defined only in terms of the dichotomy between short- and long-term information storage. On the contrary, this system has the ability to store and process information simultaneously. WM was defined (Baddeley, 1986) as comprising a number of different subsystems, each related to the specific nature of the information to be processed. In particular, it has been suggested that there is also a subsystem specialised in processing visuo-spatial information (the visuo-spatial sketch pad or scratch pad), as well as a subsystem devoted specifically to manipulating verbal information (the articulatory loop), and there is a more central component (central executive) devoted to the supervision of WM operations.

In the last 15 years, the nature and function of the WM system has been the object of a large number of studies (important overviews can be found in the books edited by Andrade, 2001, and by Miyake & Shah, 1999). In particular, the relationship between central and peripheral components and between working and long-term memory systems has been investigated and developed in a variety of recent theoretical approaches.

Despite the fact that some authors (MacDonald & Christiansen, 2002; Waters & Caplan, 1996) have questioned a primary function of WM in mind operations, the WM approach assumes that the system is involved in all cases when some information must be temporarily maintained and processed, and thus is capable of performing virtually all types of cognitive task—thought, verbal comprehension, or mental imagery. However, it is also important to define each task in terms of the type of information used and type of process required. Although the concept of WM has largely developed in agreement with empirical evidence regarding verbal processes, in recent years the number of studies investigating visuo-spatial processes has increased greatly. Additional information about the visuo-spatial sketch pad has been used to provide more information about the overall functioning of the WM. This subsystem has been called the visuo-spatial working memory (VSWM) (Cornoldi, 1995; Logie, 1995) and is characterised by the capacity to maintain visuo-spatial information in a temporary memory system and process it regardless of the stimuli source, whether perception (not only visual but also haptic or auditory) or long-term systems.

VSWM turns out to be much more complex than initially hypothesised. We have already mentioned the distinction between visual and spatial processes, and many studies have investigated the possibility of dissociating different components within spatial processing. In particular, Kosslyn (1994) showed that the components involved in processing categorical (above, below, right of, etc.) or coordinate (metric relations) spatial processes could be distinguished. Similarly, a distinction between simultaneous and sequential spatial components of VSWM has been suggested (Pazzaglia & Cornoldi, 1999). The structure of VSWM will be analysed in depth in later chapters of this book, but it is immediately evident that the dissociations reported mean that the structure of VSWM should be reconsidered. As the WM is a mechanism capable of storing and manipulating information, the approaches focused on dissociating subsystems—with regard to the specific characteristics of the information, for example visual vs. verbal or visual vs. spatial—should be integrated with those approaches that also take into consideration the nature of the process (see Cornoldi & Vecchi, 2000; Smith & Jonides, 1999).

SPATIAL PROCESSES, VISUAL MENTAL IMAGERY, AND WORKING MEMORY

This short introduction has highlighted the difficulties of identifying a common approach to investigating spatial and visual processes, mental imagery, and WM. For example, research on spatial cognition has developed along different lines, either focused on the subject's peripersonal space or focused on knowledge of larger environmental contexts. In general, research on space cognition has reinforced the idea of a close link between motor and spatial processes, whereas traditional imagery research has underlined the close relationship between memory and visualisation or between perception and mental representations.

Visual imagery can be defined as a mental process with output in an internal visuo-spatial representation, maintained and processed within a temporary memory store. If we accept this operational definition it is evident that both planning and control of movements and high-level perceptual processes require mental imagery. However, an important issue is whether to interpret mental imagery as a surrogate of visual perception or as a memory representation, and to integrate this concept in a general model of functions.

We suggest that mental imagery and visuo-spatial processes should be considered part of memory functions or, more specifically, WM functions. The basic notion of WM—as a system devoted to storing and manipulating information—makes it possible to interpret the different cognitive functions in terms of the nature of the information and the characteristics of the process. The common ground of research on spatial cognition and mental imagery is the study of internal representations characterised by the presence of both visual and spatial features. The extent to which these different features are present may vary as a function of the specific task to be performed.

However, an internal mental representation is necessary, for example, when storing information about the external world in a map-like format, visualising objects and scenes, performing tasks such as mental scanning or mental rotation, or coordinating motor activities and finding one's way in small- or large-scale environments.

In the various situations, different sorts of information are elaborated to generate an internal representation based on visuo-spatial characteristics. The possibility of integrating different information is therefore extremely important, as is the degree to which this integration is required. VSWM provides a theoretical framework that can be used to interpret different visuo-spatial processes. Mental imagery can be interpreted as a WM function. Mental images can be used to perform many different tasks but, regardless of their use, their generation, maintenance, and manipulation are functions that can be ascribed to VSWM and also, according to some proposals (Duff & Logie, 2001; Pearson, De Beni & Cornoldi, 2001), to the central executive component of WM. At the same time, simpler and less organised representations used for motor activity are likely to be an outcome of VSWM. It is necessary to specify the characteristics of this complex system and how it is possible to conceptualise a cognitive model of VSWM (and WM as a whole) that takes into account both extreme (verbal and visuo-spatial components) and minor differences (for example the distinction between visual and spatial processes). In this volume we will explore these issues on the basis of the results of research into individual differences in VSWM.

CHAPTER ONE

The study of individual differences in visuo-spatial abilities

THE STUDY OF INDIVIDUAL DIFFERENCES

An impressive corpus of data regarding individual differences in spatial cognition has been compiled in psychological research. However, these data refer to different research traditions, methods, objectives, and conceptualisations so it is therefore difficult to examine them within a single perspective.

We think that research on psychological functioning may be greatly assisted by further knowledge of individual differences. For example, analyses of individual differences may recognise the existence of independent cognitive systems in cases where a missing (or particularly important) component does not imply a deficit (or talent) in other components (for a discussion of the logic of dissociation, see Shallice, 1988). It would also make it possible to recognise the relationship between different components or forms of adaptation where a difference in one component is reflected, in the overall population or in specific groups of individuals, in differences in one or more associated components (or forms of adaptation) rather than others (for the philosophy of grouping systems and the analysis of individual differences, see Carroll, 1993). It might also make it possible to recognise aspects of psychological functioning that may be more sensitive from a differential point of view and would therefore have a greater probability of presenting variations caused by defect and "excess," and to a greater extent. However, we cannot assume that all aspects of psychological functioning are susceptible to differentiation; therefore, for those that are not, it is clear that an approach based on analysing individual differences is not useful.

In utilising data on individual differences, analyses of single cases are as important as research on groups assumed to present common elements that make them different from other groups. The study of single cases has been greatly valued in the field of neuropsychology. In particular, it has been observed that a severe selective disturbance presents a specificity that would be levelled if included in a wider group of cases with apparently similar symptomatology but different specific selective disturbances. However, the study of single cases is not entirely without the risk of describing a configuration not representative of typical human psychological functioning or demonstrating the independent nature of components that in fact normally operate conjointly. The study of groups has the advantage of being able to generalise and repeat the observations obtained with other subjects from similar populations, as well as allowing the use of certain methodologies (e.g., correlational analyses between subjects) that are obviously not possible with single subjects. It also offers information on the physiognomy of groups and therefore makes a contribution towards knowledge of the mechanism, and also an understanding of the characteristics of the population concerned.

The field of spatial ability would appear to be particularly appropriate for adopting methods of analysing differences between groups, in that well-defined and clear-cut differences have been found between well-specified distinct groups (see Vecchi, Phillips, & Cornoldi, 2001). To our way of seeing things, these differences are enlightening in their recognition of characteristics that are fundamental to the particular groups and because of the possibility of individuating visuo-spatial mechanisms, which are important and of general interest to human psychological functioning. In turn, analysing single cases with specific spatial disturbances has made it possible to recognise articulations and developments of the psychological functioning and to make a fine discrimination between mechanisms that can potentially be dissociated (even if normally they are not).

As we saw in the Introduction, research into space, mental imagery, and VSWM has taken partially diverging paths and therefore examining individual differences in this field could develop in different ways. Some analyses of visuo-spatial ability have not only involved spatial representations but also related perceptive and attentive abilities. Although the aim of this book is to examine the representations in VSWM, it cannot ignore the fact that individual perceptive–attentive-type differences may be predictors of differences in representative capacity. For example, in a review of the subject, Beaumont (1988) included them together within a global visuo-spatial skill, differentiating them from other types of ability.

THE SPECIFICITY OF VISUO-SPATIAL ABILITY

In theorising on intellectual ability, the differentiation of intelligence into different components, as opposed to considering it as unitary, has turned out to be more popular and more capable of explaining individual diversity and critical dissociations, differences between groups, and the limited correlation between measures of intelligence. These elements are all evidence in favour of a multi-component view of intelligence, which assumes that it comprises a series of components that can be distinguished, at least in part.

Within this differentiation, there has always been a place for visuo-spatial ability, either isolated as a single component or articulated to varying extents. Evidence emerges from various sources and in particular neuro-psychological research (for a review, see Nichelli, 1999), traditional psychometric research (Carroll, 1993; Thurstone, 1938), and more precisely experimental research (Friedman & Miyake, 2000; Miyake, Friedman, Emerson, Witzki, & Howerter, 2000; Shah & Miyake, 1996).

Even tests aimed at measuring intelligence correspond to these different tendencies. Two popular tests of intelligence have highlighted visuo-spatial ability in particular. The first of these is the Primary Mental Abilities (PMA) test (Thurstone & Thurstone, 1947) aimed at measuring the different intellectual components individuated by systematic use of factorial analyses. It recognises a specific visuo-spatial ability and also a specific ability of perceptive speed in certain age groups. Another test, or series of tests, is associated with the name Wechsler (1944, 1945, 1949, 1981). The scales in these tests, comprising many subtests, are based on the distinction between verbal and performance intelligence. This second test mainly examines visuo-spatial ability (the "Block Design", "Object Assembly" and, in part, "Picture Completion" subtests). The correlation between spatial intelligence scores and other types of intelligence is positive, but never particularly high, as would perhaps be expected if the intellectual mechanisms implied are basically the same (Carroll, 1993).

Although we are concerned here with human psychology, it is interesting to note how experiments with animals have led to the identification of specific areas involved in visuo-spatial elaboration that are found to be similar in humans. For example, Nichelli (1999) refers to positron emission tomography (PET) data obtained by Jonides and colleagues (Jonides, Smith, Koeppe, & Awh, 1993) and magnetic resonance data from Stein and colleagues (Stein et al., 1995) concerning simultaneous and short-term spatial memory. Subjects had to study a cross at the centre of a screen for half a second and then memorise the positions of three points (presented for 200 ms). A circle appeared after 3s and subjects were asked to decide if it was in a position previously occupied by one of the three points. It was noted that the task also activated the prefrontal cortex area of the right hemisphere (Brodman area

47), which corresponds to the region that Goldman-Rakic (1987) identified as being involved in a similar type of memory in monkeys.

THE SPECIFICITY OF VISUO-SPATIAL COMPONENTS OF WORKING MEMORY

Many studies of visuo-spatial abilities do not consider perceptive and memory components separately. This association seems reasonable from a more general point of view, in that specific characterisations at one level also involve those at another. In fact, the mnestic representation is directly, or at least indirectly, anchored to the perceptive–attentive elaboration and this is based on a representation of memory, as has been demonstrated for object recognition (Kosslyn, 1994), for example. Selective loss of the capacity to elaborate colours, space, visual stimuli, and spatial unilateral neglect may involve the perceptive level as much as the representative (Nichelli, 1999).

However, there are three valid reasons why the level of mnestic representation should be considered specifically. The first is that the two levels (perceptive and representative) do not always proceed together. For example, memory representations may be generated from information not directly corresponding to perceptual inputs. The second reason is that the mnestic level highlights types of cognitive request that do not have an equivalent on the strictly perceptive level (e.g., sequential memory) or that on the perceptive level make such simple requests that they are not generally sensitive to an analysis of individual differences (as happens in many memory tasks). The third reason is that an analysis aimed directly at understanding memory mechanisms must keep track of data emerging on this level, since perception is not concerned with the same mechanisms.

Numerous experimental neuropsychological and psychometric examinations test for the possibility of distinguishing between the perceptive and representative levels. On the psychological level it has been observed that mechanisms and perceptive phenomena do not necessarily correspond to the imaginative level (Cornoldi et al., 1998; Giusberti, Cornoldi, De Beni, & Massironi, 1992, 1998). Similar evidence has been obtained on the developmental level by observing an evolutive trajectory that is greatly accelerated for the perceptive, compared with representative, abilities (Cornoldi et al., 1998). Referring to the elderly, it has been observed, for example, that differences in old age in tasks requiring subjects to copy complex figures, such as the Rey–Osterrieth test, were mainly due to reduced accuracy in drawing; and that differences in memory were mainly the result of omission rather than distortion in the drawing (Hartman & Potter, 1998).

On the neuropsychological level, specific disturbances of memory have been demonstrated. Milner (1971), for example, described cases of disturbance to the right hemisphere where a good score for copying the Rey–Taylor complex figure could be associated to poor mnestic reproduction.

Various cases have been reported in which good perceptive activity, for example recognising objects, is not accompanied by a corresponding imaginative capacity (Farah, 1984; Grossi, Orsini, Madafferi, & Listti, 1986). Or, even more surprisingly, a good representative ability, described as success in drawing objects based on memory, was not accompanied by a corresponding ability to recognise the same objects (Behrmann, Moscovitch, & Winocur, 1994). In schizophrenic patients, specific VSWM disturbances have been found that are not associated with problems in basic perceptive ability (Fleming, Goldberg, Binks, & Randolph, 1997).

On a psychometric level, perceptive, attentive, spatial, and mnestic components have often been considered as distinct. Thurstone and Thurstone (1947), for example, distinguished between a factor underlying perceptual speed as opposed to a spatial ability component.

Various studies in this field have highlighted how representative visuo-spatial abilities depend on VSWM functioning. For example, Shah and Miyake (1996), using an interference paradigm, showed that both the storage and elaboration components of the VSWM are important for predicting spatial thinking ability. Cornoldi, Dalla Vecchia, and Tressoldi (1995) have compared children with high and low visuo-spatial abilities, but matched for other characteristics, and found specific deficits of VSWM in the former. Allen and colleagues (Allen, Kirasic, Dobson, Long, & Beck, 1996) proposed that spatial–sequential memory contributes to mediating between general spatial ability and Euclidean direction knowledge.

INTER-INDIVIDUAL (AND INTRA-INDIVIDUAL) VARIABILITY AND INTELLECTUAL FUNCTIONING

A problem met in multicomponent theories of intelligence is individuating the way these components are organised. This problem has been faced by the various theoretical positions, which we will briefly consider here.

The psychometric tradition has arisen from hierarchical factorial analysis methods that led to individuating different levels of ability. In this light, the visuo-spatial ability is not found at the central level but among the more important abilities immediately below it, hierarchically higher than more specific abilities. It must be added that, although the central level generally seems to be considered as amodal, elaboration of visuo-spatial information seems to imply central levels of elaboration. This is probably because there is a greater likelihood of presenting new and original situations requiring central control functions from the working memory (Just & Carpenter, 1992) and use of possessed knowledge is allowed less. For example, the test considered as the best measure of the central "g" factor of intelligence, i.e., Raven's

Progressive Matrices (Carroll, 1993), has visuo-spatial components that ask subjects to examine an interrupted series of configurations to identify which figure could conclude the series. It has been found that increased variability in the test scores in relation to ageing mainly concerns the spatial, rather than other abilities, suggesting that certain domains of intelligence are susceptible to variation with age (Christensen et al., 1999).

From a psychobiological point of view, it is logical to expect that the most central functions in man are those corresponding to the processes (and underlying biological structures) that differentiate man from lesser species. On the level of neurological anatomy, the prefrontal areas of the brain (and corresponding executive functions) become strong candidates for differentiation. However, visuo-spatial abilities appear to be positioned in a specific niche without great evolutionary psychological meaning, so that lesser species appear to be endowed with great visuo-spatial ability, as required for correct orientation, for example. However, it is necessary to clarify that these abilities involve only some aspects of visuo-spatial competence, and not others (such as the generation and manipulation of mental images).

Neuropsychology has also suggested the existence of hierarchically superior intellectual functions, corresponding to regions of the brain that involve wider areas and connection systems, with slower and delayed maturation in man that, if compromised, will severely affect psychological functioning. Once again, the prefrontal areas and associated psychological functions appear to be prime candidates for central functions, while the visuo-spatial functions are important but, if compromised, do not impede normal life. In any case, there is growing evidence of important implications of the prefrontal area and hippocampus in VSWM tasks (Hampson, Simeral, & Deadwyler, 1999).

The developmental perspective considers in a similar way the functions that require more time to mature and are decisive to the completion of intellectual development. The idea that visual abilities are already well developed in children has become a type of refrain that, although well-based in certain aspects (Bruner, Busiek, & Minturn, 1952; Hasher & Zacks, 1979), cannot be generalised to cover all aspects of visuo-spatial memory (see Chapter 5).

Testing groups with particular intellectual deficits (some groups will be discussed more systematically in the following chapters) confirms that most serious and pervasive intellectual deficits (mental retardation and dementia) do not generally involve a specific modality of elaboration, for example verbal rather than visuo-spatial or vice versa, but more general control systems. Nevertheless, other groups of subjects seem to have specific deficits that involve more or less central functions. It has been shown, for example, that disabled children may present specific verbal working memory deficits in reading, but that these deficits may be very peripheral in the case of decoding problems, such as modal developmental dyslexia, and more central in comprehension problems (De Beni, Palladino, Pazzaglia, & Cornoldi, 1998). A similar point will be advanced later when discussing visuo-spatial deficits.

CLASSIFICATION OF VISUO-SPATIAL ABILITIES

The differentiation and classification of visuo-spatial abilities has taken place alongside the preparation of tools to examine these abilities, sometimes inspiring, sometimes influenced by results obtained with the same instruments. For example, it is obvious that the individuation of specific visuo-spatial factors is linked to the instruments that have been chosen to examine the ability. Table 1.1 presents a list of visuo-spatial abilities outlined by studies or reviews, with a brief description and reference to the measuring instruments. It should be noted that the groupings we propose are based only on analogies and partial findings, and are open to criticism. Many tests (or associated aspects) that are in part similar, and therefore grouped under the same heading, can be separated in some cases. Table 1.1 will be integrated by a presentation of the more important instruments for examining individual differences in visuo-spatial working memory in the following paragraphs.

In recent years there have been various attempts to group the abilities presented in Table 1.1 into categories that could lead more easily to the VSWM model. In particular, a differentiation between tasks requiring passive memory of stimuli vs. tasks requiring active elaboration of material has been proposed. We have already seen the importance of this classification to an understanding of the general functioning of the working memory and it must be underlined that much of the experimental evidence in this regard has been gathered by investigating visuo-spatial abilities.

Visual memory tasks, as well as sequential and simultaneous short-term memory visual reconstruction tasks, can be classified as passive tasks. On the contrary, imagery manipulation or integration are considered as active tasks. Within this perspective, we have paid considerable attention to distinguishing between active and passive tasks, with the intention of developing a battery of tests that would reflect this distinction as faithfully as possible. Here we report some of the tasks that appear to be most appropriate for investigating these aspects of differentiation between active and passive processes, and which have been used in the experimental research described in the following chapters.

EXAMINATION OF INDIVIDUAL DIFFERENCES
IN VSWM

Some visuo-spatial subabilities specifically involve memory representations and concern the capacity to retain visuo-spatial information and/or to work

Table 1.1
Some fundamental visuo-spatial abilities

Ability	Description	Tests/measuring instruments
Visual organisation	The ability to organise incomplete, not perfectly visible or fragmented patterns	Street Completion test (Street, 1931), Embedded Figures test (Witkin, Oltman, Raskin, & Karp, 1971), Hooper Visual Organisation test (Hooper, 1958), WAIS Object Assembly (Wechsler, 1944)
Planned visual scanning	The ability to scan a visual configuration rapidly and efficiently to reach a particular goal	Elithorn's Perceptual Maze test (Elithorn, Jones, Kerr, & Lee, 1964), Trail-making test (Spreen & Strauss, 1991)
Spatial orientation	The ability to perceive and recall a particular spatial orientation or be able to orient oneself generally in space	Judgement of Line Orientation (Benton, Hamsher, Varney, & Spreen, 1983)
Visual reconstructive ability	The ability to reconstruct a pattern (by drawing or using elements provided) on the basis of a given model	Koh's Blocks (see Block Design subtest in the WAIS and WISC tests; Wechsler, 1945), Bender Gestalt test (Bender, 1938), Benton Visual Retention test (Benton, 1960), Complex Figure test (Rey, 1941)
Imagery generation ability	The ability to generate vivid visuo-spatial mental images quickly	VVIQ[a] (Marks, 1972)
Imagery manipulation ability	The ability to manipulate a visuo-spatial mental image in order to transform or evaluate it	Mental Rotation test (Vandenberg & Kuse, 1978), Spatial Subtest of DAT[b] (Bennett, Seashore, & Wesman, 1954)
Spatial sequential short-term memory	The ability to remember a sequence of different locations	Corsi test (Milner, 1971), Tomal Subtests (Reynolds & Bigler, 1996)
Visuo-spatial simultaneous short-term memory	The ability to remember different locations presented simultaneously	Visual Pattern test (Della Sala, Gray, Baddeley, & Wilson, 1997)
Visual memory	The ability to remember visual information	Contribution of memory in the Complex Figure test (Rey, 1941)
Long-term spatial memory	The ability to maintain spatial information over long periods of time	Spatial Labyrinth (Milner, 1971)

[a] VVIQ = Vividness of Visual Imagery Questionnaire.
[b] DAT = Differential Aptitude Tests.

on information held in the memory. We will discuss here, in greater detail, the most important ones involving VSWM processes.

In this field, a preliminary word of warning is necessary about evaluating the components involved. Above all, an equitable assessment of at least some spatial abilities requires determining experiential history and learning rates, as has been observed with authority elsewhere (Law, Pellegrino, & Hunt, 1993). Furthermore, identification of the instruments should be associated with an accurate knowledge of their psychometric properties, an aspect that is not always adequately considered. The relationship between the different tests used in this field should also be noted. For example, Postma and colleagues (Postma & De Haan, 1996; Postma, Izendoorn, & De Haan, 1998) highlighted how correlations between different tests—all supposed to measure the same VSWM components—can be surprisingly low. It must be noted that the reliability of specific memory tests can also be very low (around .40, according to an earlier estimate; Cornoldi, 1975), and this may partially explain the previous results.

A wide range of instruments is available to the cognitive psychologist wishing to evaluate WM, or more precisely VSWM. The review by Oberauer, Sub, Schulze, Wilhelm, and Wittmann (2000) (which also individuated a specific VSWM factor) reports 23 different tasks. The battery used in our laboratory includes a similar number of tests involving VSWM, or the elaboration of images. Some standardised batteries of memory tests (e.g., the TOMAL; Reynolds & Bigler, 1996) also include more than one VSWM test.

A common procedure for examining individual differences is based on the self-terminating principle, already included in the classic number span (e.g., Wechsler, 1944). The individual's WM capacity is tested by increasing the memory request until the subject is no longer able to repeat the information immediately and correctly (and, in some cases, in the correct order). For example, in the digit span, subjects are initially examined for their ability to remember three numbers in the correct order. If successful, they are then tested with sequences of four numbers, and so on until a point is reached where the subject is no longer able to supply the correct answer in one or two trials of the same level of complexity. If we assume that subjects face this difficulty with sequences of seven numbers—after at least one sequence of six numbers has been repeated correctly—we could conclude that the subject's span of immediate memory of numbers is six (the score evaluation system may vary slightly in some cases).

Although the self-terminating span procedure has problems (e.g., it tends to underestimate specific memory capacity because prolonged testing with different sequences tends to determine an increase in proactive interference due to preceding series; see Lustig, May, & Hasher, 2001), it is advantageous for various reasons. First, it can be administered easily, generally requiring little time. Second, it does not put pressure on subjects in difficulty, involving them in tests that are too complex (as can happen when pre-organised material must be administered). The risk is to compromise the positive attitude and perception of self-efficacy towards the whole test, including, therefore, items within the subjects' capacity. Third, the resulting score is generally self-evident to the examiner, can be computed immediately, and does not require consultation of references and manuals.

We will now describe in detail the main tasks we use to investigate VSWM. The advantages of applying a span procedure are numerous and, for this reason, the tasks have been set out with items at increasing levels of difficulty, even if in many cases (mainly for experimental and nonclinical reasons) it is generally preferred to use experimental batteries in which the manipulation of variables is more articulated.

The Corsi Block Test

The best-known procedure based on the self-terminating span principle is known as the Corsi test, named after Brenda Milner's young collaborator (Corsi, 1972; Milner, 1971) who devised a procedure similar to a classic memory span—the Knox test—that, as Richardson documented (2002; Vecchi & Richardson, 2001), was already in use at the beginning of the twentieth century to evaluate the intellectual efficiency of migrants arriving in America. If the immigrant did not perform efficiently, there was the risk of being sent back to Europe. The test was then adopted widely in neuropsychological practice and then in other areas of psychology (see De Renzi & Nichelli, 1975; Kessels, Van Zandvoort, Postma, Kappelle, & De Haan, 2000).

Figure 1.1 shows the configuration used for the Corsi test. The cubes are numbered on the examiner's side (who can therefore present the pattern required and check the correctness of the response). During the presentation phase, the examiner progressively indicates positions and then asks the sub-

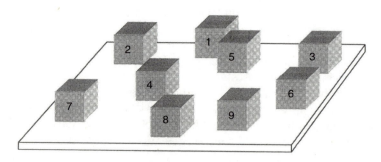

Figure 1.1.   Wooden board and cubes used for the Corsi test.

ject to repeat the sequence. Typically, the various positions are presented as a sequence—an ideal pathway—without the examiner having to lift his/her hand completely after each position (for a discussion of the different procedures used with Corsi test, see Berch, Krikorian, & Huha, 1998). Recently, the test has been proposed with some new elements, for example, a computerised version with obvious further implications about the process (role of the vertical dimension, absence of the continuity element—the hand movement—between one position and the next, etc.).

Numerous empirical tests have shown that the Corsi test measures a WM component that can be clearly distinguished from other components, in particular from the articulatory auditory components. Other research has validated the procedure, showing the relationship between this and other memory, and everyday life tasks. We have found, for example, that subjects selected for their normal number span and high scores in the Corsi test are characterised by a better memory of film (Conte, Cornoldi, Pazzaglia, & Sanavio, 1995), pathway descriptions (Pazzaglia & Cornoldi, 1999), and specific sensitivity to VSWM task interference effects when elaborating multimedia messages (Gyselinck, Ehrlich, Cornoldi, De Beni, & Dubois, 2000).

A "backwards" version of the Corsi test has also been created, similar to the "backwards digit span," which requires memorising a presentation of numbers in the inverse order. Similarly, in the "Backwards Corsi test" subjects are asked to indicate the positions starting from the last and going back to the first. The analogy with the "Backwards Digit Span" is, however, only partial because inverting the order of a spatial sequence is easier (because it is a type of "return journey") than inverting the order of a sequence of linguistic material presented auditorily. For this reason the decreases in performance typically observed in the Backwards Digit Span are not present in the Backwards Corsi. Nevertheless, differences can be found and, interestingly, this can differentiate between subjects in various ways, suggesting that the two components involved are not exactly the same.

Although the Corsi test is the most widely used and is considered representative of VSWM functions, evidence regarding the fact that the test measures a specific component, which has a very limited relation with other components of the VSWM, is emerging. For example, Luzzatti and colleagues (Luzzatti, Vecchi, Agazzi, Cesa-Bianchi, & Vergani, 1998; but see also Hanley, Young, & Pearson, 1991) examined the case of a woman with a dissociation between the visual and spatial, who had considerable difficulty in a wide range of tests, but presented a dissimilar profile between scores in the Corsi and other spatial tests. In particular, it has been reported that the central executive components of WM may be implicated in the Corsi, together with motor components (Vecchi & Richardson, 2001).

The Visual Pattern Test (VPT)

The VPT was created by Della Sala, Gray, Baddeley, and Wilson in 1997, following a procedure already used by experimental research (e.g., Phillips & Christie, 1977) to examine "short-term visual memory" largely shorn of its "spatio-sequential component." This test also includes a self-terminating span procedure and is characterised by the presentation of a single matrix of increasing complexity in which 50 per cent of the boxes are outlined in black. The subject's task in the response grid, which comprises the same matrix as used in the presentation but without the outlined positions, is to indicate the positions that were marked in the presentation.

There is considerable evidence that the test does not measure the same type of ability that is measured by the Corsi test. For example, Della Sala and colleagues (Della Sala, Gray, Baddeley, Allamano, & Wilson, 1999) have presented three types of evidence. First, the two tests, administered to an adult population of varying ages, did not correlate. Second, double associations were found in brain-damaged patients. Third, the two tests were sensitive to different types of interference. Della Sala and colleagues have argued that the Corsi test measures a spatial component of the VSWM while the VPT measures a different component, which they argue is visual. Logie and Pearson (1997) also arrived at a similar conclusion. They noted how the evolutive trajectory of the two tests (or variant tests derived from them) were different. According to the authors, the VPT involves the storage component of the VSWM, which is prevalently visual (visual cache), while the Corsi test involves the operative component of the VSWM, which is prevalently spatial (inner scribe).

Consideration of the VPT as a visual test may, however, cause some perplexity, given that it implies memorising positions in space, rather than visual configurations. Pazzaglia and Cornoldi (1999) have characterised the process implied as spatial-simultaneous, distinguishing it from a sequential spatial process and a visual process. The three processes appear to be disturbed selectively, in different ways, by concurrent tasks and seem to be implied in the elaboration of different descriptions.

The differentiation between simultaneous spatial components (implied in the VPT) and a more specific visual component is also supported by the fact that some VSWM tests, involving the simultaneous presentation of an array of pictures, attribute separate scores for correct memory of the figures, and their correct spatial position, thus obtaining evidence suggesting that the two aspects do not overlap (see Cornoldi et al., 1995; Schumann-Hengsteler, 1996). An inherent difficulty in procedures aiming to examine memory of visual stimuli, real objects, or pictures is the fact that the subject cannot proceed simply by indicating a position and must therefore use a more complex form of response, such as graphic signs (as in the complex figure test, for example (Rey, 1941), in which it is possible to evaluate memory of details and positions separately), verbal responses (for this reason the test is appropriate for testing small children, especially where the verbal code is not spontaneous; see Hitch, Halliday, Schaafstal, & Heffernan, 1991), or recognition among a series of presented stimuli.

Another way of overcoming the problem is to test not so much the visual memory of the object itself but the object–position connection considered apart from the position itself. An example will illustrate the difference between pure location memory and binding memory better. Suppose that the subject must remember a series of objects on a Cartesian plane and that at a certain point on the plane there is a picture of a flower. Three possible types of memory may be found:

(1) Pure location memory: I remember that there was an object there, but I don't remember what the object was.
(2) Pure visual memory: I remember that there was a flower, but I don't remember where.
(3) Binding memory: I remember that there was a flower in that position.

There is evidence (Kessels, Postma, & De Haan, 1999) that location and binding memory are partly independent and therefore involve different components of VSWM.

The battery of VSWM tests used in our laboratories

To build a more representative battery of VSWM tests, and at the same time exploit the advantages of the self-terminating span procedure, we set up a battery of tests in our laboratory comprising instruments that are in part derived from the literature and in part re-elaborated specifically. Some tests in the battery adopt the span principle. As well as the two tests mentioned above (Corsi and VPT), the battery includes other tasks (see Table 1.2), many of which were developed to measure the ability to elaborate VSWM information actively, to fill in the gap that was evident in the literature (for a discussion of this point, see Richardson & Vecchi, 2002; Vecchi & Richardson, 2000).

The battery of tests is briefly presented here to facilitate comprehension of the experimental data that will be presented in the following chapters.

Passive matrix tasks. This category includes a variety of tasks that are similar to the VPT developed by Della Sala and colleagues. The basic structure of the task requires memorising different positions in matrices of various dimensions. After a presentation phase, in which subjects memorise the target positions, the initial stimuli are removed and subjects are presented with a blank matrix in which they have to indicate the squares previously occupied

Table 1.2
Passive and active visuo-spatial working memory (VSWM) tasks

Type of VSWM task	Test
Passive tasks	Corsi test
	Visual Pattern test
	Passive matrix tasks
	Passive matrix tasks with verbalisable pictures
	Visual span (little houses)
Active tasks	Rotated Visual Pattern test
	Pathway span
	Image generation span
	Jigsaw puzzle task
	Selective matrix task

by the targets (Conte et al., 1995; Cornoldi, Cortesi, & Preti, 1991b). In versions used for experimental purposes, the complexity of the tasks can vary greatly according to the size of the matrix (e.g., 3 × 3 vs. 5 × 5 matrices), the number of dimensions (two- or three-dimensional patterns, e.g., 3 × 3 vs. 2 × 2 × 2 matrices), the contemporary presentation of more than one matrix (e.g., a stimulus set comprising three 3 × 3 matrices), and finally the overall number of targets (Figure 1.2). The VPT has also provided a practical and easy-to-use test in a span version, which is particularly appropriate for clinical purposes.

Passive matrix tasks with verbalisable pictures (Cornoldi et al., 1997). In this test, different matrices comprising a varying number of objects are presented (Figure 1.3). A target square is defined by the presence of a nameable object (a table, an apple) and subjects have to recall the name of the object and its position. The test is a very easy task to administer and has proved to be useful with very young children, who do not use strong verbal encoding.

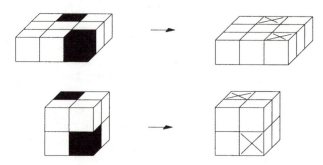

Figure 1.2. Example of material (3 × 3 and 2 × 2 × 2) matrices) used for the passive matrix tasks.

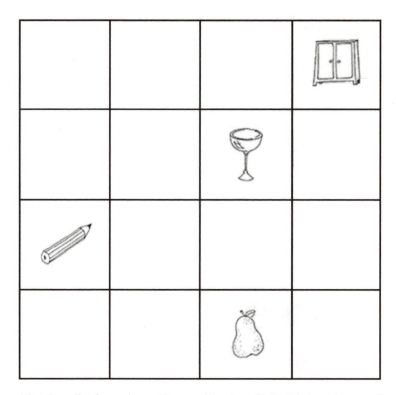

Figure 1.3. Example of a passive matrix comprising four objects (window, glass, pencil, pear).

Visual span (little houses).   In this task, originally developed by Chiara Braga in the Padova laboratory, visual stimuli are presented comprising increasing numbers of little houses of various types. Later, participants have to recognise the houses within a larger set comprising an equal number of distractors (Figure 1.4). The fact that all the stimuli share the same verbal label reduces the role of verbalisation in the performance of this task.

Rotated VPT.   This is a modification of the original VPT test in which the response matrices are presented oriented differently. Subjects therefore have to remember the original positions as well as having to rotate the configuration to be able to indicate the squares in the response matrix (Figure 1.5). This task can be interpreted as a practical active counterpart of the passive VPT.

Pathway span.   This task has often been used in association with the passive matrix task and was one of the first to be developed specifically to address active VSWM processing. Subjects are required to mentally visualise

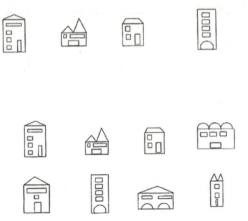

Figure 1.4.   Example of the visual span (little houses) task in a trial comprising four houses (top) that have to be recognised later within the larger set of eight (bottom).

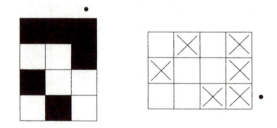

Figure 1.5.   Example of a pattern with six targets. Response matrix is rotated through 90°.

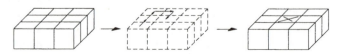

Figure 1.6.   Example of a pathway task comprising four sequential positions in a 3 × 3 matrix.

a completely blank matrix (e.g., a 5 × 5 matrix) and then to follow a pathway through a series of statements of direction (i.e., left, right, forwards, backwards). Again, the complexity of the task may vary according to the size of the matrix, the length of the pathway (i.e., number of statements), and the presence of two- or three-dimensional matrices. The combination of matrix size and number of statements has led us to propose a span version of this task in which the items are presented with increasing complexity. Figure 1.6 shows an example of a 3 × 3 matrix with a pathway consisting of four positions. In all cases, subjects have to indicate the final position of the pathway in a blank matrix.

Image generation span (Figures task).   In this task, subjects are required to generate images following verbal descriptions. Instructions ask them to visualise simple shapes (such as circles, squares, clouds, etc.) in different colours and overlapping to different extents. Five seconds later, subjects are given real coloured shapes and they have to reproduce the entire figure (Figure 1.7). Difficulty is increased by increasing the number of shapes.

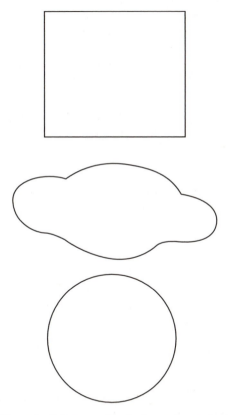

Figure 1.7.   Example of shapes used in the Image Generation task (figures).

Jigsaw puzzle task.   This task was developed by Vecchi and Richardson (2000) to provide an ecologically relevant test to assess active visuo-spatial abilities in elderly people or neuropsychological patients (a more detailed description of this procedure is given in Chapter 6). Pictures from the Snodgrass and Vanderwart (1980) set were fragmented into 4, 6, 9, 12, or 16 numbered pieces. The pieces are presented visually to subjects, together with a response sheet where they have to write down the numbers corresponding to the correct positions of the pieces (Figure 1.8). This task minimises memory load because the pieces are always in full view, but active manipulation ability is required to mentally reconstruct the picture and supply the correct solution.

Selective matrix task.   This task is a recent attempt by Cornoldi and Mammarella (submitted) to provide a visuo-spatial sibling of the Daneman and Carpenter (1980) Listening Span task (1980). Subjects are required to successively examine two, three, or four 4 × 4 matrices, and decide whether three marked squares are aligned. After having completed the task for the whole series of matrices, subjects have to indicate on a blank matrix the last square indicated in each matrix (Figure 1.9). Increasing complexity is reflected in the number of sequences presented.

DIFFERENCES IN VISUAL MENTAL IMAGERY AND VSWM DIFFERENCES

Our battery also includes visual imagery tests in which individual differences seem to be very closely linked to WM capacity. As discussed earlier, visual mental imagery is typically associated with short-term visual memory and the VSWM (Hitch, Brandimonte, & Walker, 1995; Logie, 1990). In fact most of the visual images are: (1) representations that necessarily refer to a temporary memory system; and (2) based upon analogic and semi-analogic character-istics that refer to a memory system that is appropriate for maintaining information that preserves visuo-spatial properties. It must be noted, how-ever, that there is no general agreement on the fact that mental images imply the same WM system as is involved in classic tests of immediate memory of visuo-spatial information. On the other hand, these tasks are strongly affected by secondary tasks tapping the central executive component of WM (for a discussion, see Pearson et al., 2001). These results are problematic because they would suggest reporting mental imagery operations to the cen-tral executive, which is normally considered amodal (see Baddeley, 1986), while there is a large corpus of evidence to demonstrate that mental images have a specific modal format and cannot be associated with other types of abstract representation. For example, the ability to rotate mental images appears partially independent of other central abilities (Thurstone, 1938).

However, there are alternatives to this conceptual problem. This position could be based on the assumption that the temporary memory system involved in working on images (e.g., Kosslyn's visual buffer) is distinguished from the VSWM. A different alternative (Cornoldi & Vecchi, 2000) could be to consider the VSWM system not as a unitary system, but rather differenti-

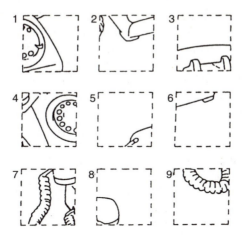

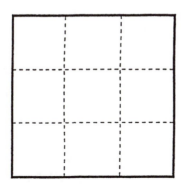

Figure 1.8. Example of a nine-piece puzzle (telephone). The blank response sheet is used to write down the correct number in the correct spatial location.

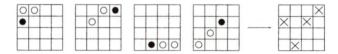

Figure 1.9. Example of a sequence of four matrices. Participants have to decide if the positions are aligned (i.e., no, no, yes, yes) and then recall the final positions on a completely blank matrix.

ated on the basis of the type of material used (e.g., visual vs. spatial) and also in relation to the amount of active control, which is higher in mental imagery than in typical visuo-spatial passive short-term memory tasks.

A third alternative could be to assume that even the most basic cognitive performance (and related tests) imply the activation of various components. Therefore complex breakdowns of VSWM and mental imagery tasks must be carried out to retrieve common and different underlying components. This alternative is followed, for example, by Kosslyn (1994) in the debate on individual differences in mental imagery. Kosslyn's suggestion is to identify the basic subsystems implied in the elaboration of mental images (Table 1.3) and to recognise those that are critically involved in each task. For example, the classic tasks of mental rotation imply the activity of numerous subsystems, the shape shift subsystem in particular.

For Kosslyn, the involvement of different subsystems would explain the correlation between different mental imagery tests. There is very little, at times even negative, correlation between these mental imagery subsystems,

Table 1.3

Subsystems posited by Kosslyn's (1994) theory of mental imagery and typical operations of those subsystems (adapted from Kosslyn, 1994)

Subsystems	Typical operation
Visual buffer	Maintains and gives basic organisation of analogical representation
Attention window	Selects regions of the representation for further processing
Stimulus-based attention shifting	Shifts to changed stimulus values (e.g., size)
Pre-processing	Extracts properties
Motion relations encoding	Detects motion patterns
Category pattern activation	Categorises processes
Exemplar pattern activation	Matches input properties with stored examplars
Spatio-topic mapping	Produces a representation, size, orientation of perceptual units
Coordinate spatial relations encoding	Computes coordinates of one unit relative to another
Categorical spatial relations encoding	Computes categorical relations between units
Associative memory	Activates associated representations
Coordinate property look-up	Accesses characteristics associated with coordinate spatial relations
Categorical property look-up	Accesses pattern code and categorical relations
Categorical coordinate conversion	Converts categorical spatial representation to coordinates
Attention shifting	Moves attention to a new location
Shape shift	Alters the representation

with an extremely varied range of correlation (Kosslyn, Brunn, Cave, & Wallach, 1984; Poltrock & Brown, 1984). An example of this approach can be found in a work by Kosslyn, Van Kleeck, and Kirby (1990a), who considered which subsystems a subject would need to be able to perform a given task and derived a measure by isolating the role of other intervening subsystems. As Kosslyn suggests, the specific measure in the critical subsystem can be derived from an analysis of variations in performance due to manipulations that are expected to affect the subsystem directly, such as task difficulty or practice in the task.

UNITS OF ANALYSIS IN THE STUDY OF INDIVIDUAL DIFFERENCES

A logic similar to that adopted by Kosslyn (1994) for analysing individual differences in mental imagery tasks could also be adopted for VSWM. For example, the Corsi Block test could be interpreted on the basis of the single operations required to carry it out, and/or the cognitive mechanisms implied. We could therefore have the following operations: representing a checkerboard (perceptual organisation mechanism), following a series of positions presented (perceptual scanning device), codifying the absolute position of an item (location encoding subsystem) and its relative position (relational encoding subsystem), storing coded information (storage system), maintenance (visual short-term memory), inhibiting irrelevant information (inhibitory mechanism), maintaining attention on the task (visual attention), and so on.

One problem with this breakdown of the task is that, even though the breakdown is fine, it cannot exclude arriving at an even more detailed breakdown. For example, the perceptive representation of the checkerboard operated by a perceptive organisation mechanism could, in turn, be broken down into a series of well-known perceptive mechanisms that lead to the construction of the object perceived (see, for example, Marr, 1982). These mechanisms are important in the study of visual perception, and can also be found in tests of single individual profiles linked to specific neuropsychological dysfunctions. It is not always certain that analogous breakdown is useful and necessary for a general reflection on the characteristics of the VSWM and implications of a particular task. With reference to the example of the Corsi Block test, an articulated breakdown of the task (perhaps even further than that proposed, to the level of the lexicon of the biochemical mechanisms underlying neuronal activity, rather than the lexicon of psychology) does not seem appropriate because it does not offer further relevant information about individual differences found in the test.

These considerations raise some problems about the definition of the most appropriate unit of analysis for a psychological explanation generally, but also more specifically for reflection on VSWM tests. Unless proven otherwise, the variance in these tests, which is normally intended to measure individual differences in VSWM, seems to refer to the variability of the VSWM. Less importance is given to a series of other mechanisms, and we will therefore refer mainly to these.

To summarise this discussion, some criteria are necessary to be able to define the most appropriate unit of analysis, and the differences found in VSWM tests in particular. These could concern the level:

(1) that meets the type of explanation required (psychological rather than philosophical or biochemical);
(2) that conciliates economy and explicative capacity;
(3) that is best able to front situations and behaviours where it is considered useful to evaluate VSWM differences (e.g., everyday memory, prediction of future behaviour, rehabilitation, etc.).

A critical issue concerns the unit of analysis. To be able to understand the organisation of VSWM through analyses of individual differences in VSWM tasks, a task analysis is necessary. This includes complex but unitarily organised operations and reflects certain basic components of the VSWM system, which is itself characterised by the presence of aspects of perception, attention, maintenance, and processing.

CONCLUDING REMARKS

In conclusion, an individual-differences approach can be useful for explaining human differences and for finding critical psychological variables that, by making individuals different, appear to be central to psychological functioning. The use of the approach must take into account its specific limitations. In particular, individual differences can derive not only from biological diversities but also from experience, motivation, and differences in strategies adopted by individuals not only in a systematic way but also in specific circumstances. These factors help to explain why highly specific cognitive tests can have rather weak psychometric properties. However, these weaknesses can be overcome either by administering multiple tests (which measure the same aspect) to single individuals and combining the results, or by the reduction of data noise obtained through the study of groups of individuals who are assumed to share common characteristics. The latter approach is the basis of this volume, which reviews evidence concerning specific groups within the human population. Obviously, the reader will only be able to get information concerning the typical patterns of performance of the considered groups, and will not be able to draw from the data inferences concerning single individuals, as the variability within those groups may be high and it is common to find subjects who present atypical patterns with respect to the group to which they belong.

The study of individual differences has been particularly important in showing the specificity of visuo-spatial abilities. Traditional studies on different forms of intelligence, and recent research on mind fractionability, have consistently shown that people high (or low) in spatial abilities do not necessarily present similar (either high or low) levels of competence in different abilities, and in particular in verbal skills. These elements apply directly to the case of WM, suggesting that the two classically (Baddeley, 1986) identified modality specific subsystems—the articulatory loop and the visuo-spatial sketch pad—can be similarly differentiated. This differentiation was clearly shown by Shah and Miyake (1996) using an individual-differences approach. In this latter study, and in a series of important succesive studies (e.g., Miyake, Friedman, Rettinger, Shah, & Hegarty, 2001), Miyake and co-authors examined the characteristics of WM on the basis of the individual differences that can be found in a randomly selected adult population. This approach follows the classical tradition concerning the differentiation of intellectual and cognitive functions (e.g., Carroll, 1993) and can be integrated by the consideration of characteristics of specific subgroups, as is shown in the present volume.

CHAPTER TWO

Models and components of visuo-spatial representation and working memory

As we outlined in the Introduction, a large body of evidence (see Logie, 1995, for a review) shows that the representation format in VSWM is specific and can be differentiated from representations in other components of WM. This format is "analogic," at least in part. It maintains some of the properties of the corresponding perceptive visuo-spatial representation and is typically associated with the phenomenological experience of having a mental image. Investigating characteristics of VSWM representation therefore implies analysing visuo-spatial processes, mental images, and their properties.

THE IMAGERY PERSPECTIVE

Despite a classical psychological reference to the concept, and some more recent pioneering work (Paivio, 1971; Shepard & Metzler, 1971) that opened the debate on the role of mental imagery in cognition, when Stephen Kosslyn began his studies on the nature of mental images in the early 1970s, very little was known about the nature of these cognitive processes, which were mainly regarded as "pictures in the head." Although this definition should not be discarded, it is evidently the product of a research tradition where the main aims were to identify, and possibly confirm, the similarities between what we see and what we imagine. Kosslyn understood that an implicit assumption needed empirical demonstration and more theorisation. In particular, he realised that it was necessary to show that so-called "mental images" had a representational format analogous to the perceptual and different from the propositional format representing either language or abstract information in memory, thus refuting criticism (Pylyshyn, 1973) of the mental imagery construct. Therefore, the real challenge was to develop experimental procedures to make possible the demonstration of the equivalence of perceptual and imagery processes. One such procedure, which was later to become one of the most important tools for investigating mental images, was "image scanning" or "mental scanning" (a complete overview of the results obtained in more than 20 years of use of this technique has recently been published by Denis & Kosslyn, 1999). The main assumption underlying the development of this procedure was that shifting attention between different parts of an image should correspond to temporal delays in direct correspondence to the metric distance between the objects, or parts of objects, to be analysed (Kosslyn, Ball, & Rieser, 1978). Characteristics of mental imagery were investigated in terms of similarity to visual perception, and the model developed by Kosslyn (1980, 1994) is strongly influenced by this theoretical perspective. Kosslyn developed his original idea of a visual buffer (1980) into a more coherent and segmented model of mental imagery (1994), in which he functionally inter-relates high-level vision and visual imagery processes. Each part of the model is designed to develop an integrated system capable of carrying out the different steps or processes involved in a variety of object-recognition conditions: recognising objects in different conditions, recognising their different shapes, recognising in poor viewing conditions, and using prototypical exemplars or objects with a larger visual scene.

A simplified version of the imagery model proposed by Kosslyn comprises seven main "boxes" that can also be fragmented into a number of subcomponents in a refined account of the model (see Kosslyn, 1994, pp. 379–383; see also Chapter 1). The visual buffer can be considered to be at the centre of this model and was described in similar terms in an account of the model presented more than 10 years earlier (1980). It constitutes a subsystem capable of maintaining spatially based information patterns, and works in conjunction with an attention window that constitutes the portion of stimuli to be selected for further manipulation. The spatial-based and object-based systems correspond to the "what" and "where" systems discussed in the next paragraph, and it is presumed that they analyse the physical properties and spatial locations of objects. An associative memory component could be considered to be the long-term storage of the information needed to identify and recognise an object, and an information look-up system guides our visual search on the basis of the information contained in long-term stores. Finally, the real attention-shifting system actually directs the focus of attention either by controlling body position or by influencing the attention window directly. (A list of the subsystems hypothesised by Kosslyn, and their functions, can be found in Table 1.3, p. 28). Although it was developed on the basis of visual perception data, Kosslyn (1994) argued that the organisation he described could account for mental imagery processes. The pattern of activation of the visual buffer could derive from visual stimuli (i.e., visual perception) or another information source (not necessarily immediate sensory inputs, such as visual imagery), but the main processes involved in the analysis and manipulation of the visual-like stimuli are similar for perception and imagery.

The relationship between mental images and perception has always been a basic theme for conceptualising the true nature of mental representations with visuo-spatial characteristics. However, at the same time the different theoretical approaches have led to hypothesising models of cognitive functioning that consider, to a greater or lesser extent, the similarity between perceptual and imaginative processes. By simplifying the problem it is certainly possible to identify two partially distinct traditions. In the first, mainly North American, the functional model is based on an analogy between perception and imagination. It is characterised by describing the imaginative system, starting from what we do when we see a scene, evaluating the distances or relationships, or simply turning the head to analyse the visual stimuli from a different angle. The other, mainly European, tradition interprets the mental image as a complex process, similar to but not the same as perception, in which the analysis, elaboration, and generation processes include not only perceptive information but also information from other sensorial sources. The semantic system also assumes a fundamental role.

This second theoretical approach considers imagery to be a representation in which memory plays a greater role. Empirical evidence concerning the "analogical" properties of mental images is incorporated in a theoretical framework in which the generation, maintenance, and manipulation of visuo-spatial representations are interpreted within the more general structure of the human cognitive system. For example, several authors have speculated on the important role played by verbal and semantic processes in visuo-spatial imagery abilities (Intons-Peterson, 1996) and the possibility of generating visuo-spatial images in the absence of any visual input (Cornoldi & Vecchi, 2000). These ideas, based on experimental findings, have led to mental imagery being considered within a broader theoretical framework, in which perceptual visual stimuli still play a role but the relationship between different components of a processing memory system are taken into account to a greater extent.

These issues are related to the distinction between an immediate memory visual trace (VT) and a generated image (GI) (Cornoldi et al., 1998; see Table 2.1). Both VT and GI are representations in VSWM, but they reflect different operations, as a VT is derived directly from a very recent visual experience and shares many properties with visual perception whereas a GI is the result

Table 2.1
Differences between two types of visuo-spatial working memory representations:
a mental image generated from long-term information and a visual trace directly
derived from visual experience (adapted from Cornoldi et al., 1998). Reprinted
with permission.

	Visual trace (VT)	*Generated image (GI)*
Access	Directly received	Generated
Attention	Very low (often pre-attentive)	High
Represented object	Phenomenic object	Constructed object
Perception analogy	Almost complete	Partial
Main characteristics	Sensorial–phenomenological properties	Selected perceptual–conceptual properties
Role of long-term memory	Marginal	Substantial
Process penetrability	Almost none	Substantial
Modality of loss	Same as sensorial information	Same as elaborated information
Interference	Visual similarity	Representation requiring similar processes
		Different processes requiring attention
Capacity limitations	Limits of storage	Limits of storage and operator
Memory variation as a function of age development	Minimal	Substantial

of a constructive process in working memory, using long-term information from different sources. Its representational format is specific not only with respect to verbal, conceptual, and propositional formats, but also with respect to the perceptual format of visual traces. For example, a GI is not affected by typical primitive perceptual phenomena (e.g., pop-out, illusions; Giusberti et al., 1992, 1998) or similarity (Cornoldi, Rigoni, Tressoldi, & Vio, 1999), but is more interpreted and more penetrable.

Our distinction between a VT and a GI seems to offer a framework for interpreting a series of events related to visual memory and mental imagery. However it must not be interpreted rigidly, as the distinction between the two is not strict but is probably continuous. As Chambers and Reisberg (1985) and a series of other studies have shown (for a review, see Cornoldi, Logie, Brandimonte, Kaufmann, & Reisberg, 1996a), VTs can also be interpreted, at least partially, and some related effects can also be found in traces stored in long-term memory. However, Brandimonte and collaborators, in an impressive series of studies (Brandimonte, Hitch, & Bishop, 1992a, 1992b), have shown that interpretation of a visual trace can be reduced by blocking the "overshadowing" mechanism induced by verbalisation, thus confirming the specificity of a visual trace.

VISUAL PATHWAYS AND MENTAL IMAGERY

Ungerleider and Mishkin (1982), studying the visual cortex of monkeys, have shown that it is possible to distinguish between two cortical visual pathways; one involved in analysing where an object is and the other in recognising the object and understanding what it is. These two neural pathways are connected with object vision and spatial processing. From an anatomical point of view, both pathways originate in the primary visual cortex, diverging at the prestriate cortex and then proceeding ventrally through the inferior temporal cortex, or dorsally through the inferior parietal cortex, respectively. It is important to consider that these two circuits are both necessary for visual elaboration of a scene, although they convey different information. The ventral pathway conveys object information and the dorsal pathway spatial information. Subsequent research based on this distinction has confirmed Ungerleider and Mishkin's early results, and has also suggested that a similar organisation could be present in humans (Haxby et al., 1991; Ungerleider & Haxby, 1994), not only in the case of visual perception but also when analysing higher processes such as mental imagery or VSWM (Courtney, Ungerleider, Keil, & Haxby, 1996). This idea is entirely consistent with a theoretical framework that assumes the equivalence of perception and imagery and, more generally, with the underlying assumption that mental imagery could be a synonym for high-level vision.

The first attempt to integrate the neurophysiological findings of Ungerleider and Mishkin in an imagery paradigm is attributed to Martha Farah and her colleagues, who began investigating this dissociation in human patients soon after the suggestion of separating "what" and "where" neural pathways. In an initial study reported in 1984, Levine, Warach, and Farah hypothesised the existence of two "visual" systems in mental imagery ("what" and "where"). Several years later, a deeper analysis of one of the two patients originally described confirmed that the impairment in the analysis of object characteristics could occur in association with a flawless performance in tasks requiring analysis of the spatial position of objects (Farah et al., 1988). In this study, the theoretical framework used by the authors was slightly different from that used by Ungerleider and Mishkin, or by the authors themselves in previous years. In fact, the distinction between "what" and "where" is now proposed in terms of dissociation between visual and spatial processes in mental imagery. The double dissociation between visual and spatial processes has been completed only recently with the report of a patient presenting the opposite pattern, that is, selective impairment in spatial elaboration in conjunction with preserved normal visual imagery processes (Luzzatti et al., 1998).

Within the WM research tradition, Baddeley and Logie (Baddeley, 1986; Logie, 1986, 1989, 1995) have also been working on conceptualisations of visuo-spatial processing in which the main assumption is the existence of separate components for analysing visual and spatial information. In recent years, the possibility of interpreting data for a specialised spatial system in a working memory framework has been further developed (Courtney, Petit, Maisog, Ungerleider, & Haxby, 1998), although the parallel possibility concerning the association of object analysis to visual working memory has not received similar treatment. The existence of a specific "what" component has been postulated repeatedly, often in association with the existence of further encapsulated cognitive processes for the analysis of other characteristics of visual stimuli, such as "when" a stimulus has been presented (Cabeza et al., 1997).

VISUAL, SPATIAL, AND MOTOR PROCESSES

An alternative way of interpreting the relationship between visual and spatial processes has been proposed by Milner and Goodale (1995; Goodale & Milner, 1992). In 1988, Livingstone and Hubel hypothesised a functional and anatomical distinction between magno- and parvo-cellular pathways within the visual perceptual system. Given the similarities with Ungerleider and Mishkin's approach, it was soon suggested that the "what" and "where" distinction could originate from magno/parvo segregation. However, subsequent observations (Milner & Goodale, 1995) suggest that both ventral and dorsal pathways receive information from what were originally called the magno and parvo pathways. A peripheral segregation (magno vs. parvo) does not seem to match a cortical distinction exactly.

Given these premises, Milner and Goodale (1995) went on to propose a functional model of the dorsal and ventral streams. Compared with the earlier models of Ungerleider and Mishkin (1982) and Livingstone and Hubel (1988), the main aim was not only to focus on characteristics of perceptual stimuli, implying a cortical segregation based on these characteristics only, but also to take the use of the information into account. In other words, Milner and Goodale underlined the importance of considering the cognitive process the information is used for, and suggested that a task-related/process-related distinction could be more useful for interpreting separate cortical pathways in high-level vision. In particular, Milner and Goodale (1995; Goodale, Meenan, Bulthoff, Nicolle, Murphy, & Racicot, 1994) demonstrated the difference between perception of an object and motor actions associated with the same object. Similar peripheral visual information is used in very different ways in conjunction with the process requirements. The requirements for visual identification of an object are clearly different from those needed to move towards the object or to extend a hand to touch it.

The authors' idea (Milner & Goodale, 1995) is therefore that the dorsal system is specifically organised to control movements and to integrate the visual information necessary to move in the environment and organise reaching and grasping behaviour towards various objects. However, the ventral system is concerned with analysing visual stimuli involving material stored in the long-term memory ("representations of the enduring characteristics of objects" in the authors' words) or, generally, the generation of perceptual and cognitive representations.

It is clear that this approach is still based on a perceptual point of view, but there is a hint of the importance of distinguishing mental structures on the basis of task characteristics, and not only on the basis of different types of stimuli. Within this framework, the use of perceptual stimuli is the key variable in interpreting elaboration in the dorsal or ventral streams. The consequences are also important for cognitive models of mental imagery and VSWM. On the one hand, it can be suggested that a mental representation is a cognitive representation of an object's enduring characteristics: The perceptual information needed to generate mental images should be guaranteed by the ventral pathway. On the other hand, it is clear that some sort of mental image also has to be generated in the case of motor guidance, although different in level of detail and visual analysis. Moreover, there is widespread evidence that motor activity, such as tapping, can disrupt VSWM processes (see Logie, 1995).

WORKING MEMORY

When studying the relationship between memory and mental imagery, two different aspects should be considered: (1) the characteristics of a memory/working memory system comprising a specific visuo-spatial processing component; and (2) the relationship between this system and long-term memory stores. Both issues have been addressed by the development of the working memory (WM) model by Baddeley and Hitch (1974; Baddeley, 1986), and later by authors proposing different variations of the original structure (Cornoldi & Vecchi, 2000; Logie, 1995) or underlining the role played by long-term memory information in working memory processes (Cowan, 1988, 1995; Ericsson & Kintsch, 1995).

According to the human information approach (Atkinson & Shiffrin, 1968), an immediate memory system is used for the reproduction of information immediately after presentation, but it is even more important as a support system capable of maintaining the information needed for a large range of human activities. In keeping with this view, Baddeley and co-authors (Baddeley, 1986) proposed a model of information processing in which the main assumption is to consider short-term memory as a system for the temporary storage and processing of information. In an impressive series of studies, Baddeley and colleagues tested the basic hypothesis and main implications of their model. In particular, in the first study in this series, Baddeley and Hitch (1974) used a dual-task technique requiring their subjects to hold a certain quantity of material (a series of two to eight digits) in short-term memory, absorbing most of their immediate memory capacity. At the same time they were asked to perform another task (learning, reasoning, or comprehending). Results showed that increases in WM load reduced performance correspondingly, confirming the WM hypothesis. However, the mind was able to execute the required concurrent cognitive task even when the entire WM capacity was absorbed by the digit memory task. On the basis of these and other data, Baddeley (1986) abandoned the assumption of a unitary short-term memory system, hypothesising that the limits of digit span may involve a WM subsystem, leaving other components of WM relatively unimpaired.

In these terms, it is important to consider the type of information that has access to the system and, of course, the nature of the task to be carried out by the system. Three separate components have been suggested for the architecture of the WM system: (1) an articulatory loop dealing with verbal material (e.g., in the immediate memory of digits); (2) a visuo-spatial sketch (scratch) pad for maintaining visuo-spatial information; and (3) a central executive with control and supervising functions, also involved in complex cognitive tasks like reasoning and comprehending (Figure 2.1).

The role of visuo-spatial processing in the system has been studied less, and this is reflected in the limited research carried out on visuo-spatial processes until the 1990s. The visuo-spatial subsystem was mainly viewed as a

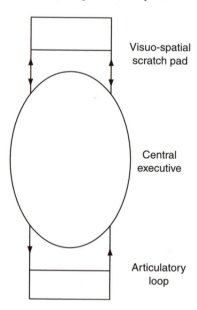

Visuo-spatial
scratch pad

Central
executive

Articulatory
loop

Figure 2.1.   A simplified representation of the working memory (WM) model (from Baddeley, 1990). Reprinted with permission.

sibling of the phonological–articulatory loop for which, on the contrary, a long tradition of research has developed. The WM model was originally developed on the basis of evidence available about the functioning of verbal subsystems. In particular, Baddeley and co-authors studied a series of effects involving the phonological–articulatory loop, suggesting that it can be articulated into two subcomponents: (1) a storage subcomponent (the phonological store) maintaining the information in a phonological format for a few seconds; and (2) an articulatory subcomponent recoding nonauditory information in an articulatory format and refreshing information maintained in the phonological store.

In particular, there are four effects regarding the phonological–articulatory loop, contributing to its articulation. The first (the phonological similarity effect) concerns the disruptive effects on memory produced by the presence of phonologically similar material. The second (the unattended speech effect) regards memory loss caused by presenting spoken material that the subject is explicitly invited to disregard. These two effects involve mainly the phonological store: In fact its phonological format is particularly sensitive to phonological similarities and access to the system is mandatory and out of the subject's control. The third (the word-length effect) is due to the lower recall of longer compared with shorter words, possibly because of the greater time required to articulate and then refresh the longer words in memory. Finally, the fourth effect, or series of effects, is due to a block of the articulation rehearsal (articulation suppression effects), which changes the patterns of performance related to the articulatory subcomponent, for example reducing or eliminating the word-length effect.

Over recent years, many effects and conceptualisations related to the original analyses of WM have been developed and also questioned. For example, some important developments concern the structure of the visuo-spatial subsystem, the function of the central amodal component, and the relationship with long-term memory.

From different perspectives, Cowan (1995) and Ericsson and Kintsch (1995) have suggested that WM should be interpreted as the activated portion of long-term memory (LTM), or that at least a portion of WM should coincide with information contained in LTM used for each specific task. These theories are very interesting because they allow one of the main issues in the understanding of WM functioning to be addressed, namely the capacity issue.

Several WM tasks require the activation of enormous amounts of information, which cannot be predicted within a traditional short-term working memory capacity. However, in our opinion, while proposing interesting ideas addressing the capacity issue, these approaches still present a number of aspects that are difficult to interpret. For example, if we think of WM as an activated portion of LTM only, then it becomes difficult to explain how we carry out WM tasks, such as mental calculations or abstract figure rotations, or deciding if the new sofa would fit well in the sitting room. These tasks require the use of new stimuli from the outside world (the new sofa is not in our LTM) that do not have to be stored in a specific LTM system but can be forgotten after a very short time interval. In other words, if we think of a WM model as a portion of LTM, how can the information used in a WM process not coincide with the information contained in LTM? Conversely, how can WM temporary output be forgotten in a few seconds? More recently, Baddeley (Baddeley & Andrade, 2000) has taken his position further, suggesting the existence of a new WM subsystem—the episodic buffer—responsible for connections with episodic LTM.

Logie's approach (Logie, 1995) to the model proposed by Baddeley and Hitch is more conservative, although his speculations have led to interesting suggestions concerning the structure of the visuo-spatial component and the relationship between WM and long-term stores. A sequence of studies carried out in the late 1980s led Logie to first consider the visuo-spatial subsystem as much more complex than previously hypothesised, and second to propose an architecture of the visuo-spatial sketch pad or visuo-spatial working memory (VSWM) divided in different subcomponents, similar to the data obtained for the articulatory loop (Logie, 1986, 1989). In particular, Logie and Marchetti (1991) suggested that visual and spatial components could be distinguished within VSWM. Later, Logie (1995) also suggested that the visual component works in a way similar to the phonological storage system of the phonological–articulatory loop, while the spatial component can be considered a mechanism of active rehearsal like the phonological–articulatory loop (Figure 2.2).

Further, Logie proposed a different relationship between WM and LTM. Baddeley's original model (1986) suggested that semantic knowledge could intervene in a WM process. Logie (1995) proposed that LTM is directly involved in the case of stimuli entering the WM system from the external world. Thus, all information manipulated in WM comes from LTM, either directly or indirectly. From a certain point of view, Logie's position attributes greater importance to the object recognition process (like Kosslyn), also extending this approach to the whole set of information processed in WM.

In an impressive book presenting different models of working memory, Miyake and Shah (1999) reviewed the main questions concerning the study of working memory under the following headings:

(1) Basic mechanisms and representation in WM;
(2) The control and regulation of WM;
(3) The unitary vs. nonunitary nature of WM;
(4) The nature of WM limitations;
(5) The role of WM in complex cognitive activities;

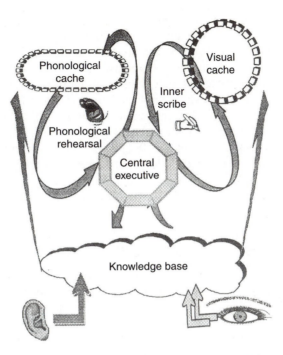

Figure 2.2. The representation of the modified working memory (WM) model proposed by Logie (1995). Reprinted with permission.

(6) The relationship of WM to LTM and knowledge;
(7) The relationship of WM to attention and consciousness;
(8) The biological implementation of WM.

Several years later, Miyake (2001) coordinated a special forum on WM from an individual differences perspective, which examined the nature of individual and age-related differences tapped by active WM spans. In particular, Miyake posed the following question: What do WM span tasks really measure and what makes them better predictors of people's performance in complex cognitive tasks than more passive, storage-oriented span tasks?

According to Miyake (2001), four alternative positions are proposed. The first alternative (the so-called resource-sharing model) posits a trade-off between storage and processing. Increased ability to process a particular type of information determines a saving in resources to be used for storing information (Daneman & Carpenter, 1980). This view has been adopted in particular to explain developmental progress in the memory spans (Case, 1985). A second view (the "controlled attention" model; Engle, Kane, & Tuholski, 1999a; Kane, Bleckley, Conway, & Engle, 2001) assumes that WM capacity is jointly determined by short-term memory capacity and the efficiency of an amodal central ability of "controlled" attention. According to Miyake, this view is compatible with the Baddeley's (1986) tripartite model of WM, assuming that WM capacity is determined by the combination of capacities of the slave systems and the central executive component. A third view (the "task-switching hypothesis"; Hitch, Towse, & Hutton, 2001) assumes that low performances in WM tasks are not only due to trade-offs between storage and processing but also to difficulty in switching from storage functions to processing, and vice versa. A fourth view (the "inhibition-based account"; Hasher & Zacks, 1988; Lustig et al., 2001) assumes that individual differences may be due to different efficiency levels of a specific inhibitory mechanism, which inhibits irrelevant information and, more generally, counters the effects of proactive interference caused by items memorised in previous span task trials.

VISUO-SPATIAL WORKING MEMORY

A temporary specific visuo-spatial memory system can be defined on the basis of the assumptions (Logie, 1995) that it receives information from either the senses or long-term memory, it is subject to a process by which information is lost over time, and it maintains information in a specific format that is related to characteristics of the visual and spatial material with which the system has to deal. Furthermore, in the WM perspective, it is also necessary for the system to be able to elaborate the stored information, which may then be used in a variety of complex human activities such as orientation, movement in space, mental imagery, drawing, and so on. These requirements produce a critical distinction between basic studies on short-term visual memory and VSWM.

There is a long-standing tradition of research concerning immediate visual memory. The human memory seems capable of maintaining a great amount of information for a very short period of time (Sperling, 1960), while still being capable of holding part of it in a transitory memory system for tenths of a second, even when the subject does not have the possibility of refreshing it (Kroll, 1975). These capacities are not specific to human beings, as they can also be found in animals. Furthermore, infants aged less than a year also demonstrate good and quite stable visual memory abilities, remembering more than one element in a series of visual stimuli presented serially, and their performance is influenced by recency effects (Rose, Feldman, & Jankowski, 2001). The characteristics and capacity limitations of visual memory appear to be related to the organisational properties of perception, although some specific elements emerge (Massironi, Rocchi, & Cornoldi, 2001; Saariluoma, 1994). In particular, Jiang, Olson, and Chun (2000) showed that visual short-term memory stores relational information between individual items on the basis of global spatial configuration. Although partially independent systems can be advocated for processing locations, colours, and shapes, an integrated type of elaboration may be required for binding different stimulus properties. The formation of a memory configuration is also modulated by both top-down and bottom-up attentional factors (Jiang et al., 2000).

Different effects may be associated with systems that do not overlap perfectly, as differences in materials, instructions, presentation modality, and retention intervals in particular may induce the activity of cognitive systems that only partially overlap. In particular (Atkinson & Shiffrin, 1968), a difference between a sensory visual register and a short-term memory store has been underlined. The sensory register maintains a large quantity of visual information in a substantially unprocessed format for a few hundredths of a second, as shown in Sperling's (1960) classical study, using the partial report technique and sensory processes like visual masking to produce memory disruption. The short-term store has limited capacity, maintains information already elaborated, and for a greater period of time, which can be prolonged further if adequate active processes are carried out (Tversky, 1969, 1974). Due to the temporal characteristics and limitations of the sensory register, the system cannot be heavily involved in WM operations that are mainly related to the activity of a visual short-term memory system. However, differences between the two systems are not always clear-cut and each may be differentiated further. Assuming that a VSWM subsystem is part of a general working memory system and operates at a functional level, mirroring the functions of a linguistic working memory (LWM) subsystem, within some theoretical perspectives it could be appropriate to study the characteristics of VSWM starting from what is known about LWM (Cornoldi, 1995; Logie, 1989; see Table 2.2), keeping in mind that the approach must be used with caution.

Visual similarity effects have been demonstrated in a series of studies with children (Hitch, Halliday, Schaafstal, & Schraagen, 1988) and adults, although it has been suggested that the disruptive effects of similarity may only affect recall of presentation order of visual stimuli (Avons & Mason, 1999).

The interference produced by irrelevant visual stimuli on VSWM operations (mental imagery activity in particular) was originally shown by Logie (1986) and then developed in an impressive series of studies by Quinn and co-authors (Quinn & McConnell, 1996; McConnell & Quinn, 2000), who examined the role of several boundary conditions for emergence of the effect.

The effect of quantity of material is also evident in VSWM as shown by Kerr (1987), Vecchi and colleagues (Vecchi, Monticelli, & Cornoldi, 1995) and Kemps (1999), for example. As these authors argue, visual complexity could be affected by different types of manipulation and is particularly sensitive to the structural properties of the material. For example, using matrix-type

Table 2.2

Potential similarities between visuo-spatial working memory (VSWM) and linguistic working memory (LWM) subsystem (adapted from Cornoldi, 1995)

Architecture	LWM	VSWM
Storage component	Phonological store	Visuo-spatial store
Processing components		
for maintenance	Articulatory loop	Rehearsal process
for elaboration	Active linguistic	Active visuo-spatial
Effects		
Similarity	Phonological	Visual (and spatial?)
Unattended information	Speech	Visual information
Quantity	Word length	Visual complexity
Disruptive concurrent activity	Articulatory suppression	Spatial tapping
Functions	Word learning	Spatial orientation
	Reading	Visualisation

material it can be shown that VSWM is affected by the number of positions to be remembered within a matrix, the complexity of the matrix, and the number of matrices that must be processed at the same time. Furthermore, as mentioned above, organised structures inducing regularity or groupings between elements can reduce the actual memory load. Specific stimulus features may also facilitate visual memory; for example, Walker, Hitch, Dewhurst, Whiteley, and Brandimonte (1997) demonstrated an impairment in image combination when the figures to be combined were incongruent in colour, but not when their grounds were incongruently coloured. The study of VSWM capacity is further complicated by the fact that memorisation of spatial locations seems to involve fewer capacity problems than other more complex visual stimuli. For example, Lee and Chun (2001) suggested that in some conditions the number of spatial locations has no effect on memory, and memory of objects associated with those locations may be more critical, concluding that the units of VSWM capacity are represented by integrated objects.

In the VSWM, a spatial tapping task inducing disruptive effects that mirror those produced by articulatory suppression on LWM has become very popular (Logie, 1995; Smyth et al., 1988). In a standard procedure, spatial tapping requires the subject to tap on a table with one hand following a particular simple pathway (e.g., a quadrilateral defined by four buttons). Spatial tapping also has disruptive effects on VSWM when carried out without vision of the buttons, but only if the movement is under the subject's control and involves a spatial representation (Quinn & Ralston, 1986). These results confirm the general relationship between spatial movements and

VSWM activity (see also Chieffi & Allport, 1997; Lawrence, Myerson, Oonk, & Abrams, 2001).

Although strong evidence (for a review, see Baddeley, 1986) has shown that a VSWM subsystem can be distinguished from other WM subsystems, contradictory results have sometimes been reported concerning the specific involvement of VSWM, or other subsystems, in a variety of tasks, including some that are typically associated with VSWM, such as mental imagery tasks (Pearson et al., 2001). For example, Salway and Logie (1995) used the classical Brooks tasks (Brooks, 1968) requiring subjects to memorise either a spatial description or a parallel verbal sequence of words. They found that the two tasks were disrupted by concurrent spatial tapping or articulatory suppression. However, a concurrent task requiring the generation of a random series of elements, typically disrupting central executive subsystem activity, also interfered with the spatial Brooks task, suggesting that the latter system may also be involved. Similar interfering effects of random generation tasks on a series of visuo-spatial and mental imagery tasks have been described in other studies, raising particular doubts about the overlap of VSWM and an "imagery buffer," i.e., a temporary system involved in processing visual mental images (for a debate, see Logie, 1990; Morton & Morris, 1995; Pearson et al., 2001). This debate, however, does not contradict the more general result that VSWM is involved in a large range of human activities such as drawing (Fastame, Cornoldi, & Vecchi, 2001), mechanical reasoning (Sims & Hegarty, 1997), multi-media processing (Gyselinck et al., 2000), spatial orientation (Denis, Daniel, Fontaine, & Pazzaglia, 2001b; Garden, Cornoldi, & Logie, 2001), and memorisation of films (Conte & Cornoldi, 1997) for example.

The articulation of VSWM

Articulation of VSWM is required by both conceptual analysis and empirical evidence. In fact, a deeper consideration of visuo-spatial processes reveals substantial differences that are further supported by empirical data. Some of these differences were mentioned in Chapter 1, with reference to the variables measured in some typical VSWM tests. Other differences, in particular the physiological basis for a distinction between visual and spatial processes, were highlighted in the first part of this chapter. Pickering (2001) reviewed literature showing that visuo-spatial working must be fractionated; she also argued that, although neuropsychological and neuroanatomical evidence is offering elements in favour of such a fractionation (as illustrated by Carlesimo, Perri, Turriziani, Tomaiuolo, & Caltagirone, 2001, and by Mendez, 2001), the correct description of the fractionated components can be premature if not adequately corroborated by a cognitive analysis.

As the following chapters show, an analysis of individual differences is

Table 2.3
Important differentiations within visuo-spatial working memory

---

Spatial sequential vs. spatial simultaneous
Spatial categorical vs. spatial coordinate
Spatial egocentric vs. spatial allocentric
Visual vs. spatial
Memory for different visual properties (colour, meaningful and nonsense shapes, texture, faces, shadows, etc.)
Memory for different visual properties affected by a spatial relation (size, orientation, binding shape and location, spatial relations suggesting a shape, etc.)
Visual detail vs. visual global

---

particularly illuminating for the fixation of different VSWM components. Table 2.3 offers a list of important differentiations within VSWM. The first differentiation mentioned has already been discussed in the first part of the chapter. Despite its intuitive appeal, specification of the distinct features of spatial and visual representations is not easy, as confirmed by the fact that the same stimulus (e.g., a matrix with a series of filled squares) has been differently interpreted as a pattern that is either visual or that describes spatial relationships (see also Chapter 1). The latter view, which represents our own position (Pazzaglia & Cornoldi, 1999), is developed in Table 2.4, which offers a series of specifications for the differentiation between visual and spatial, and between spatial sequential and spatial simultaneous. Table 2.4 also offers specifications for the distinction proposed by Kosslyn (1994) between coordinate spatial and categorical spatial. This distinction refers to the fact that spatial representations may have stronger analogical continuous properties and be processed mainly by the right hemisphere, or also involve reference to categorised discrete relationships (an object can be inside or outside, to the left or right, but cannot assume intermediate conditions) and be mainly processed by the left hemisphere (this pattern of data has been discussed by Trojano et al., 2002).

Returning to Table 2.3, it must be noted that not all differentiations are at the same level. Spatial simultaneous vs. sequential, on the one hand, is a differentiation within the spatial dimension distinct from the visual (although spatial simultaneity appears closer to the visual pole than spatial sequentiality) and coordinate spatial vs. categorical spatial, on the other, can be considered in the same way, although they seem to concern simultaneous spatiality more than sequential spatiality. Similarly, allocentric and egocentric representations are referred to as spatial but not visual representations.

At the opposite end, other differentiations regard visual representations. Both neuropsychological dissociations (see Denes & Pizzamiglio, 1999, for extensive reviews) and experimental studies (Engelkamp, Zimmer, & De Vega, 2001; Marr, 1982) show that it is possible to distinguish between the encoding

Table 2.4
Main specifications of some important distinctions within visuo-spatial
working memory

Spatial	*Visual*
More related to movement	More static
More active	More passive
Object location	Shape
Relationship between objects	Colour
Position with reference to the observer	Texture
Sequentiality of exploration is critical	Unitary perception of the form is critical
Coordinate spatial	*Categorical spatial*
Metric relationships	Categorisable relationships (connected/
Size	disconnected; left/right; inside/outside;
Orientation	above/below)
Distribution of values is dense, continuous	
High detail	
	Distribution of values is discrete
	Low details, representation of general aspects
Sequential spatial	*Simultaneous spatial*
Spatial positions presented sequentially	Spatial positions perceived simultaneously
Memory of preceding positions	May involve the perception of visual patterns
(Modest) degree of activity is required	May be processed at very low levels of activity

processes of different visual features such as colour, shape, texture, faces, and so on. These encoding processes can be considered as separate but also as integrated in processes binding two types of information that involve the same visual modality (e.g., a shape of a particular colour), and also a visual and spatial modality (e.g., a shape with a particular location). Another differentiation within the visual domain that appears particularly relevant is the encoding of either the local or global features of a pattern. A typical example is the encoding of a global pattern (e.g., a large letter "T") made up of a series of local patterns (e.g., a series of small letters "L" producing the global "T"). Several studies have shown that subjects' encoding may be more focused on global or local features.

CONTINUITY MODELS OF WORKING MEMORY

The assumption of a general WM system and independent subsystems in the classical WM models (Baddeley, 1986) derives from the need for specifications of cognitive architecture. These specifications could explain the differential effects of different experimental manipulations and the specific patterns of performance observed in particular groups of individuals, or in single dissociated cases. Regarding this latter result, the assumption of specific independent subsystems may be associated with a modular view of mind

(Fodor, 1983), assuming that specific computations are activated by independent hard-wired encapsulated modules. However, the WM system and its subsystems can be viewed as representatives of well-characterised groups of processes along continuous dimensions rather than as discrete entities. This view emerges from a series of theorisations about memory (Cornoldi & Vecchi, 2000; Cowan, 1995) and should probably be extended to many other distinctions in the memory field. In particular, in our view, three main continuous dimensions can be considered within the WM.

The first concerns the relationship between long- and short-term memory. In the past there has also been lively debate between dissociative and unitary theories (Melton, 1967). The debate acquired greater strength after the appearance of an approach (Cowan, 1995; Ericsson & Kintsch, 1995) assuming that WM is the activated part of long-term memory. This approach may have different specifications but it has the potential implication of assuming that activation is not a simple yes-or-no process, but that long-term memory information can be activated to different extents, varying along a continuous dimension, making the information more or less accessible to immediate retrieval. The most activated and accessible part should constitute the WM system, without precise delimitation from the other parts.

We will focus on a more systematic view regarding the two other continuous dimensions in the last chapter of the book, and will limit ourselves here to simply outlining them. The second continuous dimension concerns the modality of information processed in the so-called WM system. Despite the possibility of distinguishing at the perceptual level, between input elaboration systems for different modalities of information, the distinctions appear less clear at the memory level. Noncontinuous models of WM have focused on the more distant representational formats, such as verbal and visuo-spatial, but they may have great difficulty locating other formats. Tinti, Cornoldi, and Marscharck (1997), for example, have shown that auditory nonverbal WM processes can be located in neither a verbal auditory system nor in a general system involving nonverbal information, as their effects can be distinguished from the effects of both these systems. In a noncontinuous model of WM it should become necessary to create a new component ("auditory nonverbal working memory"), with the risk of multiplying the WM components involved in the elaboration of information that is neither verbal nor visuo-spatial. Furthermore, as is clear in Table 2.4, many different components can also be located within the visuo-spatial domain. If we assume that these components also enjoy the same independence as the other dissociated components, the distance between two spatial components should be the same as the distance between one of them and the verbal component. This conclusion is counterintuitive and against empirical evidence, as shown in Figure 2.3.

For example, Pazzaglia and Cornoldi (1999), in a study on the interfering

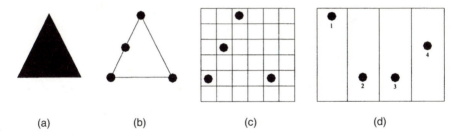

(a)   (b)   (c)   (d)

Figure 2.3.   Four cases that may be considered along a continuum moving from visual representational to spatial sequential formats. (a) A triangle resulting from the unitary organisation of several positions; (b) spatial positions in an open space; (c) spatial positions simultaneously presented in a matrix; and (d) spatial positions presented sequentially.

effects of different processes (verbal, visual, spatial simultaneous, and spatial sequential) on memory of different descriptions of the environment, found that verbal and visuo-spatial components could be distinguished better than the visuo-spatial components could be distinguished between themselves. Similarly, although two spatial components could be distinguished, overall visual and spatial processes seem to be better identified and isolated. These data suggest that the components could be located along a continuum, but leave open the question of whether the modalities should be located within a single continuum (with visual and spatial categorical components closer to language, for example) or on a continuity plane involving a series of continuous lines, with the visual component closer to the spatial, but as far from the verbal as the spatial component is.

The third dimension concerns the level of control required by the WM process. The dimension is specifically suited to locating imagery processes within the WM system. In fact, classical WM approaches interpret mental imagery as a product of a specific component specialised in processing visuo-spatial information (VSWM or a specific imagery buffer) or, if this does not apply, they associate imagery processes with the central executive component of the system (see Pearson et al., 2001, for a debate). This conclusion goes against a long-standing research tradition showing the specific analogical properties of mental images. In our view, the complexity of the processes involved in imagery abilities requires us to hypothesise a system in which peripheral modality-specific subsystems (e.g., verbal, visual, and spatial) and central amodal components are not completely dissociated.

From the point of view of a basic short-term store, one of the main differences of WM lies in its possibility to manipulate and transform information that could remain in the WM system for the time needed to perform the task. In fact, each VSWM task or operation is defined by a certain level of activity, which can be identified on the basis of an appropriate task analysis.

Table 2.5
Examples of visuo-spatial working memory (VSWM) operations
involving increasing levels of control/activity

Level of control/activity	VSWM operation
Very low level	Storage and basic maintenance of information
Low level	Basic maintenance/rehearsal mechanisms
Medium level	Generation of simple images
High level	Transformation of visual traces or mental images
Very high level	Organisation/reinterpretation of mental images

Examples of VSWM operations at different levels of activity are given in Table 2.5.

The control/activity peculiarity has been neglected in most studies on the architecture of the WM system, which have been aimed instead towards a fine-grade segmentation of the system in terms of specificity of information to be manipulated. The idea of reconsidering the architecture of the system, and the relationships between the different components, derives from the results of different studies on VSWM showing that imagery and visuo-spatial abilities imply different complex and nonoverlapping functions. In a large number of cases it is difficult to interpret visuo-spatial processes without specifying the degree of inherent control. Images can be generated from visual, tactile, verbal, or auditory information, as well as from long-term memory data, and may be manipulated, rotated, and used in association with other stimuli. It is then necessary to postulate how much control is involved in visuo-spatial tasks and what the variable affecting the request for resources may be. A more general idea of WM follows from this basis; the nature of each process is defined by the characteristics of the information being used, and at the same time, by the characteristics of the task to be performed. Several studies on individual differences (in groups of elderly, children, and blind people) have led us to consider the importance of differentiating between passive storage and active processes in WM (Cornoldi, 1995; Cornoldi & Vecchi, 2000). We have begun to believe that the degree of control required by each task could be the variable that we are looking for. This variable has allowed us to better analyse WM processes and the whole WM structure. In fact, an analysis of WM tasks in terms of the degree of activity could give important information on how peripheral modality-specific components are linked to each other, and to the central amodal processing operations.

CONCLUDING REMARKS

This chapter has reviewed some of the critical cognitive factors involved in the study of VSWM. In fact, the study of VSWM originated from the study of different psychological functions, such as short-term memory, WM, and mental imagery. Short-term memory is concerned with the temporary maintenance of information; the concept of WM includes the ability to treat that information; and mental imagery involves the representational function implied in maintaining information that is not available perceptually in analogical format. The study of these three different aspects can help to highlight the characteristics of VSWM. However, the fact that a complete study of the human mind involves the consideration not only of separate functions but also of interconnected aspects must also be taken into account. In particular, the concept of VSWM implies the involvement of the psychological functions involved in processing visuo-spatial information, from the most primitive sensory functions to more central, attentionally guided, operations. Despite the fact that the study of these aspects may enhance the comprehension of VSWM and its associated functions (as, in particular, has been shown for the study of mental imagery), visual sensation, visual perception, and visual attention will not be considered in this book, as they deserve space and focus that are beyond the scope of the present volume.

In the following chapters, we will review empirical evidence more directly focused on VSWM. In particular, we will examine evidence that helps to understand the organisation and the articulation of VSWM, with particular reference to distinctions concerning different modalities (e.g., visual vs. spatial) or between passive and active processes. This evidence has been collected over the last 20 years in a variety of individual difference paradigms. The study of individual differences has proved to be extremely fruitful in addressing this issue, also allowing us to distinguish between different sources of individual variation in the ability to actively manipulate information in VSWM.

CHAPTER THREE

Gender differences in visuo-spatial abilities

In principle, the distinction between males and females does not necessarily suggest the existence of cognitive or intellectual differences leading to the assumption that one gender is better than the other. However, for various reasons, past research in this field has followed the underlying assumption that males are "better" than females, and most of the earlier data reflects this prejudice. With a research tradition starting at the beginning of the nineteenth century (Richardson, 1997), earlier data were collected so as to confirm the male superiority prejudice. A different approach appeared at the beginning of the twentieth century and, later, the book by Maccoby and Jacklin, published in 1974, was probably the first objective overview on this topic, following the social and political transformation of the 1960s.

Before giving a brief account of this issue, it is important to clarify the choice to use the term "gender difference" rather than "sex difference." Some authors take a precise position in this debate. For example, Kimura (1999) suggests the use of the term "sex difference" while Burr (1998) has taken the opposing view, reflecting theoretical positions in the nature/nurture debate. Data regarding the existence of psychological differences between males and females are well established. Various authors attribute these differences to either genetic or sex factors present in the newborn, while others suggest that major differences emerge at a later stage and are mainly due to personality, educational, and social factors, and that consequently the term "gender" is more appropriate. We have decided to adopt the term "gender" for its greater flexibility. However, this is not because we support the above view and

disregard empirical evidence that biological factors could have a role in producing the observed differences in a variety of cognitive tasks. In fact, it is
rather because sex hormone levels could influence the performance of males
and females in certain kinds of task, even at a very early age (Berenbaum &
Hines, 1992). Furthermore, there is empirical evidence that differences
between males and females could emerge before puberty, for example with
regard to visuo-spatial abilities (Johnson & Meade, 1987; Vederhus &
Krekling, 1996).

The nature/nurture debate reflects two extreme positions, although it is
reasonable to suggest that a biological predisposition for the development of
one ability over another could develop to different extents in conjunction
with specific experience and educational factors. Richardson (1997) gave a
brief but comprehensive overview of biological and sociocultural theories
about differences between males and females, and the possible interactions
between the two approaches. Caplan, Crawford, Hyde, and Richardson (1997)
suggested that, regardless of the adoption of a theoretical background that
favours a biological or sociocultural perspective, in most cases psychological
experiments are carried out applying a distinction between males and females
that does not take into account biological factors.

Research on gender differences started in the early nineteenth century
and it is interesting to note that the first impulse to investigate cognitive
performances of males and females was not directed towards genuine scientific development but, instead, was intended to confirm the prejudice for male
superiority (Caplan et al., 1997). Religion was losing some of its impact on
Western populations and there was a need to reaffirm male superiority in
order to maintain a clear distinction in social power and roles. "Scientific"
research was thus driven towards a specific purpose and it is interesting to
note how data coincided with this need. We should also consider that because
scientific research was a male prerogative in the late nineteenth century, this
produced further support for error and prejudice.

Since the brain is responsible for cognitive and intellectual abilities, gender
differences had to be found in its anatomy (Walker, 1850). Phrenologists
believed they had found the basis of gender differences in a lesser development of the female frontal lobes. More recently, intelligence has also
appeared to be related to development of the parietal lobes, and differences
were immediately reported in this direction. The need for scientific support
for the supposed male superiority has produced an incredible amount of
research and it is surprising to find such data even in very recent years.
Attempts have been made to relate intelligence to the weight and size of the
brain, because males tend to have a larger brain. However, this would not
explain why elephants, for example, cannot be considered more intelligent
than humans. In 1974, Haller and Haller suggested a relationship between
intelligence, weight, and height, but again this is in marked contrast to a

comparative perspective. Moreover, females seem to have a greater relative weight of the brain and it has been shown that the relative size of the brain is inversely related to absolute body weight.

Differences between the weight and size of the human brain are still being investigated (Lynn, 1994), although Haug (1987), for example, has demonstrated that a larger brain does not correspond to a greater number of neurons. Observations against a relationship between weight and intelligence were also collected in the nineteenth century, when it was noted that while lower brain weight could lead to reduced cognitive abilities, females could bear a brain weight of 32 ounces without problems, while males showed intellectual malfunctioning from a weight of 37 ounces (Mosedale, 1978). Thus, it could also be concluded that the female brain is more efficient.

Overall, these data have no scientific value but they are useful in understanding some aspects of current investigations into gender differences and artefacts that could affect research in this field.

MALES PERFORM BETTER THAN FEMALES IN VISUO-SPATIAL TASKS: A CLASSICAL VIEW

Since 1930, studies have reported significant differences between males and females in a variety of cognitive tasks, with the most important results being found in analyses of verbal, mathematical, and visuo-spatial abilities.

In 1974, the seminal work of Maccoby and Jacklin provided the first comprehensive review of the impressive number of studies on gender effect on cognitive functions. The data they reported (which have been confirmed in more recent reviews, see, for example, Richardson, 1991) outline a general pattern in which females perform better in verbal tasks and males demonstrate greater mathematical and visuo-spatial abilities. However, this seems to be an over-simplification and closer analysis is necessary to understand the real nature of gender differences in cognitive tasks. It is not possible to consider here all the studies on the interaction of gender and cognitive tasks, but a brief review of the most important studies could provide an understanding of the overall picture.

Female superiority in verbal tasks seems more evident in measurements of verbal fluency, word production (Kimura, 1999), and, to a greater extent, verbal memory (Cohen, Schaie, & Gribbin, 1977; Hyde, 1981; Maccoby & Jacklin, 1974). Although there is some discrepancy about the presence of these differences in young children (Anastasi, 1981; Kaufman & Doppelt, 1977; Maccoby & Jacklin, 1974), this advantage does not diminish with age and thus does not seem to be related to a developmental advantage (Bleecker, Bolla-Wilson, & Meyers, 1988; Feingold, 1988; Hyde & Linn, 1988; McGuinness, Olson, & Chapman, 1990).

The data are more heterogeneous for mathematics. Early reports in fact indicate a general prevalence of males in arithmetic and mathematics tasks, but a more precise assessment highlights the need for a closer analysis. Males demonstrated a greater ability to solve mathematical problems but females outscored males in calculation tasks (Jensen, 1988; Marshall & Smith, 1987). This effect does not seem to be related to teacher expectations, since data favouring males and results favouring females appeared in the same class and thus the same teachers would be responsible for the opposite effects. Furthermore, the same outcomes have been observed in different cultures and ethnic groups (Jensen, 1988; Lummis & Stevenson, 1990).

Initial results concerning visuo-spatial abilities were more straightforward, indicating a general male superiority in mental transformation and rotation tasks (Harshman, Hampson, & Berenbaum, 1983; Kail, Carter, & Pellegrino, 1979; Metzler & Shepard, 1974; Newcombe, 1982), as well as geographical orientation (Oltman, 1968) and orientation in an artificial environment such as the virtual Morris Water Task (Astur, Ortiz, & Sutherland, 1998). Interpretation of the data has identified the underlying causes of this superiority as both "nature" differences, such as levels of sex hormones or genetic factors (Broverman, Vogel, Klaiber, Majcher, Shea, & Paul, 1981; Dawson, 1972; McGee, 1979), and "nurture" differences, for example, sociocultural effects (Baenninger & Newcombe, 1989; Richardson, 1994). More recently, Casey (1996) has acknowledged the effects of both nature and nurture in determining gender outcomes in visuo-spatial processing.

META-ANALYSES CONCERNING GENDER DIFFERENCES

A clearer pattern of gender differences emerged from the advent of meta-analyses in the late 1980s. This technique integrates results obtained in several studies to give a more precise evaluation of the magnitude of the different effects and to identify the most sensitive effects (Hyde & McKinley, 1997).

In the case of verbal abilities, Hyde and Linn (1988) integrated results from more than 150 studies on gender effects in verbal abilities and, overall, the data show a much smaller general effect than was hypothesised. In several tasks (including vocabulary and essay writing) the differences were only marginal, although they were a little more reliable in tests of general verbal ability or speech production. Data support a similarity between differences at all ages. Similar results were confirmed later by Hedges and Nowell (1995), greatly reducing the general significance of the supposed female superiority in verbal abilities. However, Halpern (2000) still noted a greater incidence of developmental verbal problems in males.

Mathematical achievement has been analysed by Hyde, Fennema, and Lamon (1990). These authors did not generally support the well-established belief of a general male superiority in mathematics. Differences were often negligible and only a marginally significant difference in problem solving was found. Interestingly, the pattern of difference varied across age. The pattern in young children was the opposite; females performed better in computational tasks, while the difference favouring males emerged in adolescence for more difficult mathematical tasks. Educational and social factors seemed to play an important role in these data.

To analyse gender effect in visuo-spatial span performance, Linn and Petersen (1985), and Voyer and colleagues (Voyer, Voyer, & Bryden, 1995) carried out meta-analyses on more than 50 years of research and concluded that it was impossible to consider visuo-spatial abilities as a whole, since the effects should be analysed more precisely by distinguishing perceptually based processes and various kinds of higher-level, more demanding functions.

The distinction between passive and active manipulation in visuo-spatial tasks was of particular significance. Both Linn and Petersen (1985) and Voyer and colleagues (1995) reported that significant differences favouring males were found in tasks requiring mental rotation and manipulation of mental images only. Differences were less significant in passive tasks and sometimes were not significant at all.

This confirms the data obtained by Paivio and Harshman (1983; Harshman & Paivio, 1987) as well as the study carried out by Harshman et al. (1983). These studies show that males were better in rotation and transformation tasks but that at the same time females performed better in vividness ratings and passive recall. The female advantage was maximised when judging the visual characteristics of objects (McKelvie, 1986; Sheehan, 1967). In a theoretical account of the integration of these data, Paivio and Clark (1991) noted that gender differences emerged in dynamic imagery favouring males while more static, passive tasks led to a similar, or sometimes better, performance by females. Loring-Meier and Halpern (1999), using a series of imagery tasks, argued that the great differences favouring males in tasks requiring transformations in VSWM could be due to an underlying common speed factor.

In conclusion, meta-analyses on visuo-spatial abilities gave stronger and more reliable data on the existence of a gender difference, although the supposed male advantage seems to be confined to a selective group of functions (mental rotation and manipulation). It seems that the nature of the specific task is the variable underlying the presence of significant individual differences. These differences could be interpreted either in a conservative view, suggesting that each task produces specific outcomes, or in a broader perspective. According to the latter, tasks where gender differences can be found share some common characteristics, in particular: (1) they require active working memory processes; and (2) they involve a specific visuo-spatial modality.

According to point (1), as suggested in Chapter 2, VSWM tasks can be distinguished on the basis of the degree of "activity" required. Mental rotations and manipulations are highly active VSWM tasks that imply gender differences, whereas the simple generation of vivid low-resolution images or immediate visual memory involve less active operations and do not imply gender differences. Confirmation of this view comes from its generalisability to other tasks; in fact, another recent investigation has shown that the male advantage is highly significant, not only in rotation tasks but also in other forms of transformation, such as translation (Levine, Huttenlocher, Taylor, & Langrock, 1999).

According to point (2), females perform less well in active VSWM tasks not because of a lower ability to cope with highly active tasks in general but because of a specific visuo-spatial difficulty. This characteristic is confirmed by the high performance of females in verbal WM tasks, including the most active ones, or in other tasks associated with verbal intelligence (Hyde & Linn, 1988).

GENDER DIFFERENCES IN PASSIVE AND ACTIVE VSWM

To investigate the interaction between gender and type of task (passive vs. active), we initially decided to use a variant of the matrix tasks (see "Pathway Span" (p. 23) and "Passive Matrix Tasks" (p. 21) described in Chapter 1, in which both passive and active tasks are administered together to maximise the possibility of matching performances in the two tasks by the same group of participants; Vecchi & Girelli, 1998, Exp. 1). This task had not been used before to study gender differences but was shown to be appropriate for examining VSWM active processes (Vecchi et al., 1995).

In this condition, subjects are first presented with a passive matrix and are instructed to memorise the positions of the target cubes. They are then asked to follow a pathway in an imagined matrix of the same size as the one previously presented in the passive task. Finally, they are required to give passive and active answers in a blank matrix by indicating, first, the final position of the pathway, and second, the positions previously occupied by the target cubes. Two-dimensional (2D: 3 × 3) and three-dimensional matrices (3D: 3 × 3 × 3) were used. Passive tasks could include two or three positions whereas active tasks included pathways with three or six statements of directions (Figure 3.1). Thirty-six participants were tested, divided equally for gender and matched for age and education. We expected a significant gender effect favouring males in active task performance, while minor or no differences were expected in passive tasks. Results confirmed our hypotheses and we reported a highly significant difference between males and females in the active tasks.

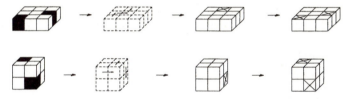

Figure 3.1. Examples of the sequential procedures involving both passive and active tasks (using either 3 × 3 or 2 × 2 × 2 matrices). Participants had to memorise the positions of the targets and then follow the pathway in an imagined matrix, point to the final position of the pathway in a completely blank matrix, and finally point to the positions previously occupied by the targets.

This result was further confirmed by the measures of effect sizes (Cohen, 1969; Richardson, 1996) of gender effects on the four different comparisons (2D vs. 3D matrices, passive vs. active tasks). Effect sizes were rather small (always less than 0.20) in the passive tasks, whereas in the active tasks they were significantly higher (always more than 0.50).

This initial study confirmed the existence of a selective gender effect in the case of active tasks while differences in passive conditions emerged only when characteristics of the material seemed to require some sort of active manipulation (3D effect). A further experiment (Vecchi & Girelli, 1998, Exp. 2) was designed to replicate and maximise the expected effects by using more complex matrices. Given the difficulties that could be induced by 3D matrices with 27 cubes (3 × 3 × 3 matrices; see Cornoldi et al., 1991b), we decided to use a more complex 2D matrix only (4 × 4). To simplify the procedure, we presented trials where passive tasks included five targets and active trials included six statements of direction only. However, we decided to investigate further the possibility that subjects were using a verbal strategy to carry out the tasks, and specifically that males and females could rely on verbal coding to different extents. Data regarding this point are rather intriguing since Vecchi (1998) reported that subjects do not use verbal strategies while carrying out this type of visuo-spatial task, but there is also evidence of gender-related preference in the type of strategies used (e.g., McGlone, 1980; Richardson, 1991). With this aim, we developed verbal siblings for the visuo-spatial tasks adopted, which were used to measure the effects of selective and nonselective interference. The verbal passive task consisted of the recall of word lists while the active task involved generating a nonsense word resulting from stringing together the initial letter of a sequence of syllables presented auditorily. Thus passive and active visuo-spatial tasks could be performed in a selective interference condition (passive and active visuo-spatial tasks together, as in the previous study), or in nonselective interference conditions (passive visuo-spatial task together with verbal active task, and passive verbal task with active visuo-spatial task). The general procedure was the same as the first study and we tested 20 participants, again divided equally for gender and matched for age and education, in passive and active visuo-spatial tasks. The verbal tasks were used as secondary tasks to analyse interfering effects. The results clearly replicated the data of the previous study. The interaction between gender and type of task was significant; males were better in the active task but no differences emerged in the passive condition.

Selective interference effects were significant (in the expected direction) in the passive task only. This result is consistent with the fact that the active task required an immediate response and was less sensitive to interference effects that, on the contrary, disrupted passive performance. However, both genders had a similar pattern of performance and this excluded a differential use of verbal strategies by males or females (Figure 3.2). Once again, analyses of effect sizes confirmed that gender effects were highly significant in the active task (values always higher than 1.00).

These two studies offer convincing evidence for the need to distinguish between passive and active visuo-spatial processes when interpreting gender differences. However, a further objection can be proposed. Since our procedure required participants to memorise the positions first and then perform the active processing tasks, it is possible that females have a general lack of system capacity or resources. As a consequence, the system could have used

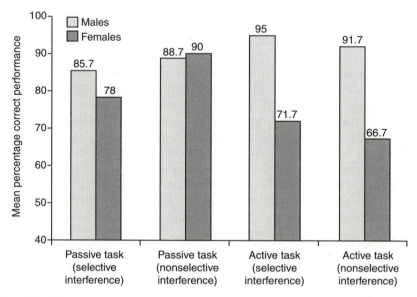

Figure 3.2. Mean percentage correct performance as a function of gender and interference condition for both passive and active visuo-spatial tasks (adapted from Vecchi & Girelli, 1998, Exp. 2). Copyright © (1998), with permission of Elsevier Science.

all its resources to carry out the passive task and the reduced capacity could cause an overload, selectively affecting active performance.

Overall, the data from these two experiments confirm that gender differences in visuo-spatial abilities may be confined to tasks requiring mental transformation or manipulation of material. Differences in passive tasks are negligible and evident only in association with tasks requiring some sort of active manipulation, as, for example, when using 3D matrices. It is interesting that while we were carrying out our studies, other authors obtained similar results. In a computerised version of an object relocation memory task, Kessels and colleagues (1999) highlighted that gender differences emerged in association with specific characteristics of the task. Males performed better than females only when integration of the material was required; the effect was not general but related to specific processing components.

MALES PERFORM BETTER THAN FEMALES IN VISUO-SPATIAL TASKS: STRUCTURAL OR STRATEGIC FACTORS?

From a general point of view it is interesting to investigate if gender-related effects are due to structural factors in the VSWM architecture or rather to strategies developed through experience and practice. There is considerable evidence to show that training could minimise gender differences (Lawton & Morrin, 1999) and, at the same time, different researchers have indicated that gender differences have diminished over the last 40 years and suggest that in the future there will be no differences at all if education levels are carefully matched (Caplan et al., 1997). However, there is also evidence that in some cases differences are not disappearing, above all when mental rotation ability is involved (Colon, Quiroga, & Juan-Espinosa, 1999, Voyer et al., 1995). This result may not appear in particular conditions. In a recent study (Frigotto & Cornoldi, 2001), we divided a large sample of young adults by randomly assigning them to a standard control condition and a relaxation + imagery condition. The two groups were matched for mental imagery abilities. In an experimental session, those in the relaxation + imagery condition were induced to relax and trained in the use of mental images. They were then invited to perform a creative imagery task (the Mental Synthesis Task proposed by Finke & Slayton, 1988) and a paper-and-pencil mental rotation test (Vandenberg & Kuse, 1978). Subjects in the control group participated in an identical experimental session, the only difference being an informal conversation instead of the initial training. Results showed that the relaxation + imagery condition group performed significantly better than the other. However, when the results were considered separately for gender, we found that the training effect applied to the female group only. In fact, the two groups, which appear to differ in the standard control condition, showing the typical male superiority effect, are not different in a relaxation + imagery condition. This result shows that male superiority in a mental imagery task may be due, at least in part, to females' poorer use of resources and strategies. Further research is necessary to demonstrate whether the females' improvement was mainly due to the relaxation component of the training (perhaps reducing the disturbing effect of anxiety when confronted with a new task and/or increasing the ability to find new strategies) or the imagery component (perhaps increasing the use of imagery strategies over the less effective verbal strategies).

The pattern is thus unclear and we are left with uncertainty about the nature of gender differences in visuo-spatial abilities. The fact that the importance of distinguishing between passive and active processes has been reported in a variety of individual difference studies raises the issue of determining whether the same underlying cause is responsible for the experimental outcomes. To investigate this issue it is necessary to select a category of subjects who are likely to show the dissociation between passive and active processes independently of the gender effect. We therefore decided to investigate gender differences in a population of congenitally blind people. As we will see in Chapter 6, the congenitally blind experience a selective deficit in visuo-spatial imagery processes in the active manipulation of images only. Thus the characteristics of their limitations are similar to those that have been discovered in gender studies. However, if it seems reasonable to postulate an experience factor to explain gender differences, a more structural approach is necessary to interpret the limits of a visuo-spatial system developed without the assistance of visual perception and on the basis of sequential information only. In other words, the sequential haptic processing of congenitally blind people may produce a different organisation of the VSWM system, which reflects a reduced performance in active tasks. Conversely, gender differences could be due to a less efficient use of strategies at least partially determined by sociocultural and developmental constraints. In principle, we cannot exclude the possibility that blindness does not produce experience effects. However, blindness and gender effects do not necessarily originate from the same differences in experience. If this is the case then the two distinct effects should combine in an additive fashion in a population of congenitally blind females. On the contrary, if a similar underlying cause is responsible for the effects observed in the two populations, then no gender effect should be reported for blind subjects. A recent study investigated this issue by analysing gender differences in congenitally blind people while controlling passive and active visuo-spatial processes (Vecchi, 2001).

Thirty-two congenitally blind participants, divided equally for gender and matched for age and education, were presented with a procedure similar to the one described above in the first experiment of the Vecchi and Girelli study (1998). Passive and active tasks were administered at the same time in a sequence comprising: (1) identifying target cubes, recognisable by touch; (2) following statements of direction; (3) active response; and (4) passive responses. The study used 2D and 3D matrices (3 × 3 and 2 × 2 × 2, respectively). The number of targets could be two or three and the number of statements of direction could be three or six. For the hypothesis to be confirmed, we were expecting an additive effect on the active tasks as a consequence of gender and blindness.

An analysis computing the variables of gender, task, and blindness shows a very clear-cut three-way interaction demonstrating the additive characteristics of the active limitations of the two groups (Table 3.1). Although both blindness and gender produced significant main effects, blind females experienced greater impairment and performance was significantly poorer than in the other conditions.

These data indicate that the hypotheses of different structural and strategic factors affecting blind and female subjects, respectively, is supported. Moreover, additional evidence comes from analyses of load factors in passive and active tasks. In passive tasks, females are selectively affected by an increase in the number of targets. An even clearer pattern emerges in an analysis of the number of statements of direction. Once again, the interaction between number of statements, gender, and blindness is significant, and Table 3.2 shows that the gender-related effect is more pronounced in the blind group, and is maximised with longer pathways.

This study has established the existence of independent factors affecting performance in visuo-spatial active tasks. A gender-related effect (lack of appropriate strategies) is associated with a blindness-related effect (different system organisation and possibly strategic factors). These data confirm the importance of distinguishing passive and active processes in VSWM and suggest that a simple distinction or dissociation is not sufficient to explain the

Table 3.1

Mean percentage of correct performance as a function of blindness and type of task for males and females (adapted from Vecchi, 2001)

	Males	Females	Effect size
Passive tasks			
Sighted	88.1	86.3	0.08
Blind	71.1	71.1	0
Active tasks			
Sighted	93.7	90.6	0.15
Blind	76.6	49.2	1.33

Measures of effect size are calculated following Cohen's method (Cohen, 1969) as reported in Richardson (1996).

Table 3.2
Mean percentage of correct performance in the active tasks only
as a function of blindness and number of statements (3 vs. 6)
for males and females (adapted from Vecchi, 2001)

	Males	Females	Effect size
Sighted			
3 statements	93.7	92.2	0.05
6 statements	93.7	89.1	0.16
Blind			
3 statements	75.0	60.9	0.49
6 statements	78.1	37.5	1.41

Measures of effect size are calculated following Cohen's method (Cohen, 1969) as reported in Richardson (1996).

complexity of the system. A poor active performance could be associated, potentially, with a variety of underlying causes, both structural and strategic.

CONCLUDING REMARKS

Although there has been a considerable number of studies on gender differences, interpretation of results often suffered from social prejudice and theoretical limitations. In the past, many empirical studies were carried out with the principal aim of confirming male superiority. Studies on gender differences have been a clear example of how prejudice and vested interest can drive research data; indeed, similar problems still arise in some investigations into individual differences that aim to confirm the purported link between intellectual ability and race.

More recently, a rigorous approach highlighted both similarities and differences between genders; the visuo-spatial domain appears to be critical in identifying gender differences, generally confirming a male advantage. However, this advantage in visuo-spatial tasks is not homogeneous: Males outperformed females in tasks requiring the manipulation and transformation of visuo-spatial material and complex imagery tasks. On the contrary, differences in passive visual memory were not significant, with some reports indicating a female advantage. Data highlight the importance of considering the passive vs. active distinction when interpreting WM processes. The nature of the process seems to be a key variable in evaluating cognitive processes. Gender effects in active tasks are specific and not comparable—in terms of underlying causes—to similar data obtained in other populations, such as congenitally blind people.

The debate concerning nature and nurture effects in determining cognitive differences between males and females is far from being resolved and it is possible to hypothesise that both biological and experiential factors affect performance. In particular, recent data suggest the importance of considering both sociocultural and genetic effects in explaining gender differences in cognitive abilities and, more specifically, in visuo-spatial functions. However, a biological determinant of gender differences seems well documented. For example, Kimura (1999) clearly demonstrated gender differences in newborn infants and a recent study comparing monozygotic and dizygotic twins (Ando, Ono, & Wright, 2001) highlighted that a large proportion of individual differences in WM abilities could be explained by genetic factors, underlying both modality-specific (verbal vs. visuo-spatial) and process-dependent effects (storage vs. manipulation).

CHAPTER FOUR

Individual differences in children's visuo-spatial working memory

The study of individual differences in children's visuo-spatial working memory (VSWM) can be considered under two main headings, which we will look at in this chapter. The first concerns age effects, including the possibility that at least some components of VSWM develop with age, and the factors underlying this development. The other heading regards the possibility that great differences in VSWM ability can be found within the same age group. This second heading can only be considered separately from a broader perspective concerning VSWM limitations within populations of all ages, both with and without specific profiles (as in particular syndromes such as Turner syndrome, see Chapter 7). In fact, some groups with specific VSWM limitations can be specifically found in developmental populations. The second part of this chapter will consider children with high verbal and low visuo-spatial intelligence who typically present a nonverbal learning disability.

THE DEVELOPMENT OF VSWM

The study of VSWM development must consider a series of preliminary questions. Two of these, regarding developmental variation and its specificity, appear to be crucial.

The first question is: Does VSWM really develop with age? In fact, anecdotal phylogenetic and ontogenetic evidence seems to suggest that animals and young children can also have very good VSWM. Many animal species have good memory for places, locations, and pathways. Children seem very good at remembering visual stimuli and locations. Habituation paradigms (e.g., Fagan, 1970) have also shown that newborn infants have very good memory for visual configurations. Young children are typically successful in tasks and games requiring memory of locations. Furthermore, they have an impressive tendency to imitate behaviours they have seen before, thus demonstrating a good memory for the behaviours. Consistent with this view, some studies have suggested that location memory shows little age change (DeLoache & Brown, 1983).

Experimental studies with animals offer a very wide pattern of data that cannot be reviewed here, although they could be of particular interest. For example, Anderson, Anthouard, de Monte, and Kempf (1993) reported that young macaques had a better VSWM than those aged 20 years or older.

Empirical studies on children's VSWM have shown great effects of age. Although some studies have suggested that certain aspects of VSWM change little in children (for example, automatic encoding of the spatial position of objects; Hasher & Zacks, 1979), other studies have shown a developmental trend even in the most basic spatial abilities. Foreman, Warry, and Murray (1990), for example, proposed a radial arm maze task for children aged between 18 and 58 months. This task required them to search for sweets among 10 identically labelled locations (placed 36° apart in a radial arrangement) in a room. On each test day, they computed the proportion of each child's choices they considered as WM errors, that is, locations visited previously in search of the reward, and found that there were clear developmental trends. The youngest children (aged between 18 and 28 months) made more errors than intermediate-aged children (33 to 42 months), and these in turn made more errors than the oldest (aged between 47 and 58 months). Other studies (e.g., Schumann-Engsteler, 1992) have shown that a similar age change in location memory can be found with older children.

Our studies have also shown that most VSWM capacities evolve with age (Conte et al., 1995). We have found, for example, that children's performance increases significantly from 7 to 11 years in a series of tasks that tap VSWM, such as recalling spatial positions or solving a jigsaw puzzle. It should be noted, however, that lower visuo-spatial memory in younger children does not imply a lesser use of the underlying systems—in fact the opposite occurs. Although imagery abilities develop with age (Kosslyn, Margolis, Barrett, Goldknopf, & Caly, 1990b), and mental images created by children under 7 years of age are mostly static, paralleling the difficulty they experience using mental imagery in reasoning (Piaget & Inhelder, 1955), young children tend more than adults to use visual representations for information processing (Kosslyn, 1980). Children's preference for a visual code has been widely pointed out and documented (Bruner, Olver, & Greenfield, 1966; Smirnov, 1966/1973), and has been applied to the specific case of VSWM. In particular Hitch and colleagues (Hitch et al., 1988, 1991) have shown that 5-year-olds, unlike older children, have a preference for visual stimulus encoding and do not use verbal coding spontaneously. For example, Hitch et al. (1988) found that 5-year-old children meet more difficulty in remembering a series of visually similar figures (like "fork" and "pen") than a series of figures whose corresponding names are long to articulate (like "umbrella" and "kangaroo"). In conclusion, a developmental trend can be observed in many VSWM tasks. However, the fact that this trend may be less evident, or even absent, in some aspects offers important information about the specificity of VSWM development and its potential differentiations from other cognitive systems. This is an important point because it contradicts the hypothesis that the development of VSWM simply reflects a more general cognitive maturation.

In fact, the second preliminary question concerns the specificity of VSWM development. In other words: Do developmental variations in VSWM reflect specific mechanisms or do they simply reflect the development of a more general underlying ability, or a common ability? This latter position is implicitly assumed by theorists who relate the development of visual memory and mental imagery abilities to intellectual development in children (Piaget & Inhelder, 1966); a position that has also been assumed by neo-Piagetian theorists. Case (1985), for example, offered an important conceptualisation of WM that distinguished its processing space into storage and operative areas. The storage space is involved in maintaining information and the operative space is devoted to the implementation of operations on that information. The total space should not vary with age, whereas developmental change should concern the proportion occupied by the two types of space. In fact, there is an increase in efficiency and automation of mental operations with age, the operative space requiring less resources, with the consequence that more resources are available for storage.

Increased efficiency of operations has also been stressed by Kail (1988), who tested children of different ages in a series of tasks, including visual search, memory search, and mental rotation, and found that the developmental change was described well by exponential functions with a common rate of change. Results were interpreted in terms of a central mechanism determining the processing speed involved in all tasks. Other theories have preferred to focus on other central mechanisms; on the inability to inhibit irrelevant information (Brainerd & Reyna, 1993; Dempster, 1993) for example, or extensive coordination between different processes (Yee, Hunt, & Pellegrino, 1991).

The study of correlation between tasks allows us to contrast two alternative hypotheses, that is, the general-resources or specific-modality nature of cognitive development. High correlation between verbal and visuo-spatial spans were found by Swanson (1993, 1996) and, more recently, by Chuah and Maybery (1999). In particular, Swanson (1996) found that tasks related to verbal WM (e.g., word span, story recall, semantic associations) and visuo-spatial WM (e.g., matrix recall, spatial position recall, memory for abstract scrawls) were generally intercorrelated in children. Chronological age (range 5–19) also correlated at an equal level with verbal and visuo-spatial WM measures. Swanson concluded that developmental improvements in WM could be attributed mainly to general capacity, and not to specific verbal or visuo-spatial processes.

These positions have the limitation of focusing on the relationship between tests, without paying enough attention to their specificity. The finding that different WM tasks are highly correlated between themselves, and age, is partly a by-product of the more general fact that all cognitive measures correlate highly with age and that correlations are typically high when based on scores obtained with subjects of a wide age range. If the same argument were applied strictly to physical development, the consequence would be to consider the different variables of growth (weight, running speed, characteristics of hair, psychological aspects, etc.) as highly correlated, and then as necessarily dependent on the same mechanism. Despite the artefact, correlational studies have also shown different patterns for verbal and visuo-spatial working memory. For example, Rubini and Cornoldi (1985), testing a group of children in a limited age range, found that forwards and backwards digit spans, together with other verbal memory tests, had a high loading on a specific verbal factor and a negative loading on a visuo-spatial factor concerning a series of visuo-spatial tasks, including the Corsi forwards and backwards tests.

If it is true that common elements associated with neurological maturation are responsible for variations in different components of cognitive functioning, including WM, then there is considerable evidence for the fact that those components deserve separate specific consideration. This evidence is based on consideration of different developmental trajectories, an analysis of dissociated patterns of performance, and also group studies. Nichelli, Bulgheroni, and Riva (2001), for example, reported that verbal and visuo-spatial span sizes were not comparable in children. Pickering, Gathercole, and Peaker (1998) examined verbal and visuo-spatial short-term memory in children aged 5 and 8 years. They found that performance was largely unrelated and concluded that the two components are dissociable. A further result of their study regards similarities in type of error (serial position, migration patterns) for the different tasks, suggesting that although verbal and visuo-spatial systems are separable, they share common processes specialised in extracting serial-order information. Other studies have focused on more active WM tasks, finding low correlations between listening span tasks (requiring subjects to select and remember only part of the processed information) and similar visuo-spatial tasks (Ehrlich, Brebion, & Tardieu, 1994; Seigneuric, Ehrlich, Oakhill, & Yuill, 2000). Further evidence concerning this point can be found in studies showing a specific relationship between VSWM and a series of everyday activities, such as spatial orientation (Conte et al., 1995), school achievement (Gathercole & Pickering, 2000), and drawing (Fastame et al., 2001), without a corresponding relationship with verbal WM. This evidence concerning the dissociability between children's verbal and visuo-spatial subsystems in WM adds to the large body of evidence already found for adults.

DIFFERENTIATION WITHIN VSWM

Efforts to differentiate development of the various components of VSWM show the specificity of the system. For example, studies in the first years of life show how primitive modalities of representation evolve and new modalities emerge. As Millar (1994, p. 254) argues, in young children "the combination of immaturity and lack of knowledge produces conditions of uncertainty. These require more informational redundancy ... typically, infants and young children require more familiarity in all aspects of tasks, more repetition, more salience (attention-getting characteristics) of cues, and more redundancy generally than required by older children and adults." For Millar, differences in spatial representation during development do not correspond to developmental stages but reflect the type of information the child can access more easily. Egocentric spatial representation is predominant in young children because self-referent coding predominates and external cues fail to elicit attention.

In older children, data comparing different age groups support the need to distinguish between different task modalities and different levels of required control. Concerning the task modality, the distinction between visual, spatial simultaneous, and spatial sequential could be critical. Logie and Pearson (1997) showed a developmental fractionation, that is, different developmental trajectories in children aged between 5 and 12 between memory for spatial sequences tested with Corsi-type procedures and memory for spatial patterns tested with procedures inspired by Della Sala and colleagues (1997) (see Chapter 1). They found that memory for patterns increased more rapidly. The ability was generally better than memory for spatial sequences for all ages, the difference being particularly evident in older ages. The authors considered the memory for patterns task as an example of visual memory, although spatial relations were very much involved. Pickering, Gathercole, Hall, and Lloyd (2001) distinguished between a static modality, where the to-be-remembered elements are presented simultaneously, and a dynamic modality, where the same elements were presented sequentially. The two modalities were used with a matrix and a maze, showing, in both cases, different developmental trajectories. Pickering (2001) argued that these results raise problems for a continuity model based on a control vertical continuum, but did not consider the fact that they are consistent with a continuity model that also assumes a differentiation along a horizontal continuum. In particular Pickering et al.'s (2001) data mirror the data obtained by Pazzaglia and Cornoldi (1999), who showed that verbal and spatial processes can be clearly distinguished, but that—within the spatial area—a further differentiation is possible between spatial simultaneous and spatial sequential processes.

More specifically, visual components have been considered by other studies, for example, by Schumann-Hengsteler (1996), who tested children's memory for objects and their location. Recently, we found a particular group of children with spina bifida who seem to present a specific deficit for visual passive VSWM components, but not for spatial components (Mammarella, Cornoldi, & Donadello, in press). Lange-Kuettner and Friederici (2000) found that memory for objects, compared with memory for locations, was specifically disrupted by visual interference in children aged between 3 and 10 years. Similar results have also been observed in a study we made with second- and fifth-graders (7 and 10 years old) (Conte et al., 1995). Children were administered a VSWM test divided into three steps, and a series of verbal WM tasks. In the first step of the VSWM test, a 5 × 5 matrix, with a variable number of cells filled, was presented for 10 s. After 5 s, the children had to indicate the filled cells on a blank matrix. In the second phase, children were administered a task (inspired by the pathway span, see Chapter 1, p. 23) using the same matrix, where they had to imagine the movement of a spot that changed position either four or six times, and then indicate the arrival cell on a blank matrix. In the third phase, the two tasks were proposed together on a 4 × 4 matrix. Children were shown the matrix with four cells filled, for 15 s. They had to follow a mental pathway and indicate the arrival cell, and then remember the four filled cells. Age differences were found in all tasks but were more evident for active than passive tasks. Furthermore, only performance in the first task was predictive of children's orientation ability when moving blindfolded in a room they had memorised just before.

Conte et al.'s (1995) study shows that developmental specifications can also be found in studies regarding mental imagery. In another study, we (Cornoldi et al., 1998, Exp. 5) found that development of the ability to maintain generated images was slower than development of visual short-term memory. Generation of mental images seems to represent a higher point in an activity continuum than the simple maintenance of visual memory. However, if children's difficulties increase in correspondence with higher points in this continuum, it should be expected that they are greater for mental imagery tasks requiring a higher level of activity. Several studies have shown that children are able to perform computationally complex visuo-spatial processing tasks, such as mental rotation (Marmor, 1975, 1977), although they require more time than adults, and can adopt strategies that are at least partially different (Lejeune, 1994). A study by Kosslyn and colleagues (Kosslyn et al., 1990b) found age differences when comparing the performance of 6-,

8-, and 14-year-olds in a battery of mental imagery tasks, such as mental rotation or generation, maintenance, and scanning of mental images, but they found that differences were less evident in tasks requiring information to be simply maintained in memory.

The capacity to perform complex VSWM tasks (e.g., mental rotation) relates to the ability to use the spatial terms "right" and "left" correctly. Benton (1959) and Corballis and Beale (1976) have shown that this ability normally develops in children between 7 and 11 years old. A similar pattern of development is evident when measuring ability to rotate letters or recognise mirror images (Braine, 1978; Vogel, 1980). Children's performance in topographical memory tasks is also poor before 8 years of age, both for orienting in a real environment and for recognising places. However, 12-year-olds perform similarly to adults (Cornell, Heth, & Alberts, 1994). The close relation between the use of "left" and "right" and the development of visuospatial ability is supported by research carried out by Roberts and Aman (1993). In this study, 6- and 8-year-old children were tested in spatial orientation and mental rotation tasks that required imagining rotation of their own bodies. Results show that only the children who were able to use the spatial terms correctly performed well in the rotation tasks, and only in these children was rotation time related to the angle of rotation, as reported in research with adults.

In relation to models of WM (Baddeley, 1994), the development of VSWM could be largely a function of increased knowledge and improved central executive functioning, as opposed to changes in subsidiary visuospatial buffers. In Piagetian terms, the unfolding of the operational stage of thought (Piaget & Inhelder, 1955) leads to a greater ability to process and transform information, and results in the development of complex visuospatial processes. However, differences in children's VSWM seem to reflect more subtle specifications, possibly based upon the active manipulation processes required by the different tasks.

DEFICITS AND EXPERTISE IN VSWM

Studies with children presenting specific deficits in visuo-spatial abilities have been very fruitful in understanding the development of VSWM. Neuropsychological and early developmental studies may offer a view of primitive mechanisms involved in the development of VSWM, but the pattern of data is still unclear. Eslinger, Biddle, Pennington, and Page (1999) presented a 4-year longitudinal study of a young boy with a deep right frontal arteriovenous malformation, who presented VSWM impairment as well as other cognitive functions, mainly executive, that were not necessarily related to VSWM. A series of studies on the effects of prenatal/perinatal focal brain injury on spatial pattern processing by Stiles (2000) highlights the difference

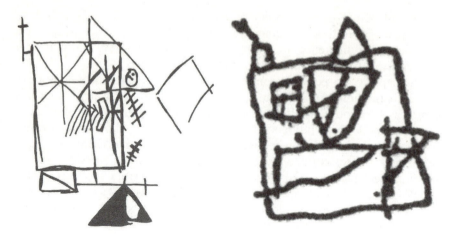

Figure 4.1. Examples of memory reproductions of the Rey's complex figure.

between the ability to recognise and represent parts of a pattern and the ability to recognise the overall configuration. This difference has also been found in clinical evidence with memory tests; for example, Figure 4.1 presents typical performance patterns from Rey's (1941) Complex Figure test. Some children have a poor memory for figures but are able to maintain the overall configuration, whereas others have a comparatively better recall of detail but less memory for the overall pattern and how the details are related to the whole.

Performance patterns with Rey's test are interesting because they clearly differentiate between spatial simultaneous and visual features, both at the molecular level (location of a detail vs. its shape) and the molar level (visual representation of the overall pattern vs. its essential spatial relationship). However, although the two aspects appear more easily distinguishable at the molecular level, this is less clear at the molar level.

CHILDREN WITH LOW VISUO-SPATIAL INTELLIGENCE AND HIGH VERBAL INTELLIGENCE

Specific patterns of VSWM performance can also be found in children with less severe problems and without explicit evidence of organic malformation. In a series of studies we examined the performance pattern of low visuo-spatial, high verbal intelligence (LVSI) children with a discrepancy between visuo-spatial intelligence and verbal intelligence, and a particular group of nonverbal learning disabled (NVLD) children where this discrepancy is associated with conspicuous school learning difficulty. The presence of groups with an LVSI profile reflects the classic differentiations within the general intelligence domain (Carroll, 1993) already considered in Chapter 1. However, the relationship between low performance in visuo-spatial intelligence tests and VSWM has never been studied in depth.

Cornoldi, Dalla Vecchia, and Tressoldi (1995) have analysed the performance of 37 low visuo-spatial intelligence children, ranging from 10 to 14 years, in a series of tasks involving VSWM. The children were selected from a large sample of more than 1000 subjects for their low visuo-spatial intelligence associated with a high verbal intelligence level. Low visuo-spatial intelligence was defined as a low performance in the spatial subtest of the PMA intelligence scale (Thurstone & Thurstone, 1947), which requires subjects to rotate and match complementary figures mentally. The results show a selective VSWM impairment in LVSI children whose visuo-spatial results were about 0.85 points lower in the Figure Intersection test (Pascual-Leone & Ijaz, 1989), which required them to find the intersecting area of an increasing number of overlapping geometrical figures. LVSI children had particular difficulty in the three VSWM tasks (memory of matrices, solving jigsaw puzzles, or following a pathway in a matrix), taken from a battery devised for testing these children (see Cornoldi et al., 1997), when their performance was compared to normal children of the same age, schooling, sociocultural level, and verbal intelligence. In particular, LVSI children presented a specific pattern of performance in the three tasks, suggesting an articulation of VSWM into subcomponents.

In the jigsaw task, three or four pieces of paper had to be joined to form a meaningful pattern, either without visual help (only the verbal label of the finished model), with the aid of the visual model, or with the model exposed for 30 s just before solving the puzzle (Figure 4.2). Compared with controls, LVSI children had particular difficulty when having to use VSWM either to remember the pattern just presented or during the back and forth movement of the eyes from the model to the puzzle pieces. However, the two groups performed similarly when they did not have to rely on VSWM. (A further unpublished control carried out by Alcetti, in our laboratory, has shown that the performance pattern is not due to specific selection of stimuli.)

The mental pathway task proposed in this study was a variation of the task already described (see Chapter 1, p. 23). Children were presented with a 4 × 4 matrix and were asked to remember two filled cells and imagine a six-position movement, visualising the movement "as a bike riding along a pathway," and then to indicate the final position. Data show that LVSI children performed less well in both subtasks, with greater difficulty in the mental pathway. Half the trials were carried out with articulatory suppression, so it was possible to examine whether the two groups were using different strategies, affected differently by the verbal concurrent task. It was found that this task disrupted the performance of the two groups to the same extent.

The matrix task required subjects to remember the names and positions of

Figure 4.2. Example of patterns (bird and cow) that have to be reconstructed from memory. Each pattern is shown for 30 s and then removed. Children are given the single pieces and they have to reconstruct the entire figure (from Cornoldi et al., 1997). Reprinted with the permission of Centro Studi Erickson, Trento, Italy.

four, six, or eight objects presented on a 4 × 4 matrix. Performance in the matrix task showed that the LVSI children's difficulty mainly reflects a problem with spatial components of working memory. Their mean number of spatial errors was more than double that of the controls, whereas the difference was smaller for visual errors. This pattern of performance could be due to the use of a verbal code for memorising objects, the use of which increases with age. More generally, it must be noted that there is no evidence that the pattern of impairment presented by LVSI children is related to a developmental delay. In fact, in the spatial tasks we found significant differences between groups but not between the two age groups.

In another study (Cornoldi & Guglielmo, 2001) we selected another group of LVSI children in a similar way (ten 9-year-olds and nine 11-year-olds) and tested them in a series of visual imagery tasks. This study showed that LVSI children's difficulties extend to a variety of imagery tasks even when they are visual. Children were administered four visual imagery tasks (the visual imagery span, interactive imagery in verbal learning, image scanning, and mental subtraction) and three verbal tasks (forward digit span, abstract triplet learning, sentence scanning). LVSI children were poorer in all imagery tasks, but not in the verbal tasks. It is important to mention that in no mental imagery task, except the visual span, did we find significant differences due to age, confirming that these abilities do not have a particularly evident developmental growth, but nevertheless can be critically impaired in some children. Figure 4.3 shows the patterns of performance for the LVSI and high visuo-spatial intelligence groups in the visuo-spatial tasks.

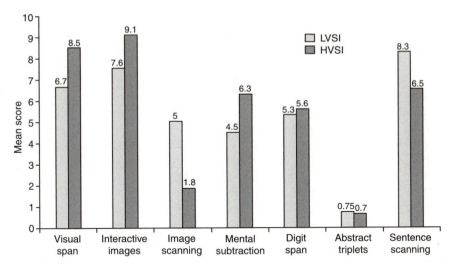

Figure 4.3. Mean scores of low visuo-spatial, high verbal intelligence (LVSI) and high visuo-spatial, high verbal intelligence (HVSI) children in visuo-spatial and verbal tasks. Image and sentence scanning performance is expressed as number of errors (adapted from Cornoldi & Guglielmo, 2001). Reprinted with the permission of The Korean Journal of Thinking and Problem Solving.

The pattern found with LVSI children was also partially replicated (Tressoldi & Cornoldi, 2000) with a group of mentally retarded children. In this study we distinguished between active and passive tasks and between visuospatial and verbal tasks, and also found that correlations were higher for tasks measuring the same component, intermediate for tasks sharing one aspect (either modality or level of activity), and lower for the more distant tasks.

THE SELECTIVE VSWM MATRIX TASK AND ROLE OF INHIBITION, INTERFERENCE, AND CONTROL

Finally, in other research with a group of LVSI children, again selected with similar but even more stringent criteria (Cornoldi, Braga, & Mammarella, 2002a), we found that LVSI children had particular difficulty in a spatial task mirroring the WM (listening or reading) span task designed by Daneman and Carpenter (1980). In the latter task, subjects had to process sentences and then select and remember only the last words of each sentence processed. This task has been successfully proposed in a large series of studies, showing its capacity to differentiate between working memory abilities and their relationship with other cognitive functions, and in particular reading comprehension ability. We developed a similar VSWM task, mirroring the main aspects of processing and selection involved in the Daneman and Carpenter (1980) WM span, the Selective Matrix task (see Chapter 1, p. 25).

We found that LVSI children had particular difficulty with the Selective Matrix task, mirroring the difficulties found by low-ability subjects in Daneman and Carpenter's task. Furthermore, this difficulty was associated with a tendency to make intrusion errors, that is, to indicate nonfinal positions, again mirroring an effect found for verbal WM (De Beni et al., 1998; Palladino, Cornoldi, De Beni, & Pazzaglia, 2001; Passolunghi, Cornoldi, & Di Liberto, 1999). In fact, errors due to nonfinal processed positions were generally more frequent than errors due to other cells, but the tendency was particularly evident in LVSI children. This result is important because it suggests that success in active VSWM tasks is partly related to the ability to exclude irrelevant information from memory, so that WM resources can be correctly allocated to proper information.

The tendency to make intrusion errors is not due to a tendency to fill the missing memory with randomly selected incorrect positions. The "intrusion" errors in this task (i.e., recall of nonfinal processed positions) are not only more frequent than errors due to completely new positions but (as another unpublished experiment with adults has shown) they are also more frequent for nonfinal positions that were more intensively processed (subjects had to tap in correspondence with some positions). Furthermore, similar effects can be found not only in LVSI children but also in other groups of subjects who have difficulty in VSWM active tasks, such as the elderly (see Chapter 5) and children with attention deficit disorder, whose deficit in control of VSWM mirrors a similar deficit in control of verbal working memory (Cornoldi, Marzocchi, Belotti, Caroli, De Meo, & Braga, in press).

Altogether, the data we obtained with LVSI children show that there is a critical relationship between VSWM and visuo-spatial intelligence, and that specific aspects of VSWM must be considered.

CHILDREN WITH NONVERBAL LEARNING DISABILITY

Learning disability (LD) refers to children with good intelligence but severe school learning difficulties. Although most LD concerns linguistic difficulties, there is a subgroup showing a pattern of good linguistic competencies associated with marked visuo-spatial difficulties. Children affected by nonverbal learning disability (NVLD) (see also Rourke, 1989) or right-hemisphere learning disability (Nichelli & Venneri, 1995) have a normal performance in verbal tasks together with poor scores in visuo-spatial and mathematical tasks, and a large discrepancy between verbal and performance (or spatial)

IQ (see also Cornoldi et al., 1999). In many respects they are comparable with LVSI children but are characterised by a more specific learning disability and, typically, by other symptoms.

Cornoldi et al. (1999) studied a group of 11 cases, aged between 7.4 and 13 years, and compared them with a matched control group. Children were administered the same matrix task proposed by Cornoldi et al. (1995) and a variation of the mental pathway task. They were also required to recall the locations of either three, four, or five positions filled on a 5 × 5 matrix and had to use interactive mental images to recall paired word associates. NVLD children performed poorly in all tasks. However, they presented the pattern of data already observed by Cornoldi et al. (1995) for the matrix task, in a particularly evident way (more errors of memory for location than memory for objects), and for the mental pathway task (particularly difficult for NVLD children also with respect to the recall of positions).

NVLD children also appear to have particular difficulty with more active tasks in an unpublished study (carried out in collaboration with F. Marconato and A. Molin) using the Corsi block span, as their performance compared with controls was lower in the backwards than in the forwards span task. Despite its simplicity, the backwards task implies a moderately higher level of activity as the child's task is not simply to repeat what has been seen but also to subject it to a certain level of activity. These data are particularly impressive as the backwards spatial span does not imply any increase in difficulty for the controls, but a severe impairment for NVLD children.

A more detailed analysis of three NVLD cases (Cornoldi, Rigoni, Venneri, & Vecchi, 2000; Rigoni, Gasparetto, & Cornoldi, 1999) reveals that each case may show a specific pattern of performance. NVLD children generally have greater difficulty with more active VSWM tasks, and this was true for two of the three cases we studied, whereas the other child presented an opposite pattern. This dissociation between passive and active competencies is very important, both to disclose the pattern of performance in NVLD children and also to suggest that it is possible to perform flawlessly in active tasks while having an impairment in passive storage functions. Enrico, who was 9 years old, failed in 9 out of 14 passive VSWM subtasks, but in only 1 of the 8 active proposed tasks. This was in particular contrast with the case of Giulia, aged 13 years, who failed in 8 of the 14 passive tasks and 6 of the 8 active tasks.

CONCLUDING REMARKS

In conclusion, the study of developmental populations appears to be particularly important for the comprehension of the nature of VSWM. Some information is offered from the study of normal development, whereas other information comes from the study of exceptional children. The two types of information do not necessarily overlap as VSWM failures may be dramatic and do not necessarily mirror developmental delays. In fact, some good VSWM competencies seem to be highly developed in very young children, while others are characterised by different developmental trends, thus producing developmental fractionations, for example distinguishing between sequential spatial and simultaneous spatial (visual) components of VSWM (Logie & Pearson, 1997; see also a similar distinction between "static" and "dynamic" processes proposed by Pickering et al., 2001) and distinguishing between a visual trace and a generated image (Cornoldi et al., 1998).

Particular genetic-based subgroups of individuals, including children, with VSWM deficits are reviewed elsewhere (see Chapter 7). In this chapter we have examined the case of two other, partially overlapping groups (i.e., children who have good verbal intelligence and low visuo-spatial intelligence (LVSI) and children with these characteristics who also have severe learning disabilities). The two groups present similar patterns of performance with severe failures in a series of VSWM tests, including visual imagery tasks. Imagery tasks, including tasks based on verbal material, appear to be associated with tests examining VSWM directly, suggesting that common cognitive structures are involved. Cornoldi et al.'s (1995) study provided evidence for the fact that difficulty in a visual task (an object reconstruction task) is dependent on VSWM, because the difference between groups is more evident when the child has to rely on VSWM to carry out the task than when the child works on the material on the basis of a simple verbal label.

Data for the pathological groups generally confirms the relevance of the passive/active distinction as the majority of children failed to a greater extent in the active tasks. A critical factor of this distinction could be associated with general cognitive development, as the active tasks appear to require more general WM resources and the quantity of general resources available to the system has been shown to be critical in explaining developmental differences (Case, 1985).

It is interesting to note that not all children with VSWM difficulties demonstrated the gap between active and passive tasks to the same extent, and we also found a case with an opposite pattern of dissociation. This case was isolated, so further evidence is needed to support the idea that certain groups of children may encounter particular difficulties with passive, but not active, tasks.

CHAPTER FIVE

Visuo-spatial working memory in ageing

The presence of a cognitive decline associated with human ageing is now well established (Craik & Salthouse, 1992, 2000). Psychometric studies in the first half of the twentieth century demonstrated empirically that performance is reduced in a variety of cognitive tasks in old age. Since then the number of studies has grown impressively, especially during the 1990s, probably as a consequence of new demographic problems related to the increasing age of the population. Understanding the modifications associated with ageing is not only a theoretical enigma—there is also a real need for both social and medical reasons. Psychological evaluation and assessment have become more and more important in investigating cognitive abilities in old age. The increasing presence of pathological conditions associated with age (such as Alzheimer-type dementia) has also determined the need for precise tools in conjunction with a more refined theoretical background.

It is not the aim of this chapter to review the enormous literature on cognitive ageing. Data showing memory decay in the elderly are reported continually, and even investigating visuo-spatial ability has become a fast-growing area. However, recent data suggest that WM is a very important structure in understanding cognitive ageing and it has been hypothesised that a variation in WM capacity is one of the main variables associated with reduced mental efficiency (Salthouse, 1994). Furthermore, both long-standing tradition and recent studies (Jenkins, Myerson, Joerding, & Hale, 2000a; Jenkins, Myerson, Hale, & Fry, 2000b) have argued that "visuo-spatial cognition" is more age-sensitive than verbal cognition. Difficulty for the elderly could be related specifically to VSWM, as it also appears when the role of visual ability is ruled out (Fahle & Daum, 1997). In addition, recent evidence has shown that cortical areas associated with WM capacity and imagery are functionally independent from areas involved in modality-specific visual processes (Raz, Briggs, Marks, & Acker, 1999).

More generally, a significant proportion of the recent theoretical interpretation of cognitive ageing suggests that it is possible to show a reduction in processing speed (see, for example, Cerella, 1990, or Salthouse, 1991) and, at the same time, a reduction in frontal, executive abilities. The literature on these aspects is very broad and, whereas the majority of researchers tend to confirm the importance of identifying unique factors in cognitive ageing (Frieske & Park, 1999; Verhaeghen & De Meersman, 1998), or even a combination of both frontal decline and response slowing (Maylor, Vousden & Brown, 1999), other authors suggest that it is difficult to falsify the common factor models (Allen et al., 2001) and that it is rather premature to relate all cognitive effects on ageing to a unique mechanism (for a review of the different positions, see Dixon & Hertzog, 1996). Data on central, frontal decrement associated with cognitive ageing have also been used to explain the hypothesised reduction in performance in the dual-task condition in elderly people (de Ribaupierre & Ludwig, 2000; McDowd & Shaw, 2000). This reduction is evident even when the disrupting task does not require large amounts of cognitive resources, such as in the study reported by Lindenberger, Marsiske, and Baltes (2000), which simply required subjects to walk and compared them with conditions in which participants were sitting or standing.

Another important aspect of cognitive ageing is connected with the effects of experience. Data reported by Salthouse and colleagues (Salthouse, 1991; Salthouse, Babcock, Skovronek, Mitchell, & Palmon, 1990) indicated that experience and ageing could be considered to be independent factors, the former related to the level of expertise determining performance while the latter produced the cognitive decay associated with old age. More recent data tend to question this hypothesis (Hultsch, Hertzog, Small, & Dixon, 1999; Masunaga & Horn, 2001) and to suggest that age-related decline could be diminished as a function of intensive practice. However, it is still possibile that everyday intellectual activities and competencies could be associated with cognitive efficiency in high-ability individuals until age-related decay limits daily activities.

MODIFICATION OF VSWM IN AGEING

In a general perspective, empirical studies investigating visuo-spatial abilities in a life-span paradigm have always indicated that elderly people show a more or less critical reduction in performance. However, the gap between young and older adults is not homogeneous, but varies depending on the task.

Initial studies showed that there is a selectively more pronounced decay in visuo-spatial, compared with verbal, abilities (Arenberg, 1978). These data partially reflect the absence of appropriate tools for measuring visuo-spatial processing, compared with verbal abilities, and the fact that existing visuo-spatial tasks are often more difficult to understand, complex, and unfamiliar to subjects than the corresponding verbal ones. In fact, numerous studies have indicated lack of familiarity and other context-dependent factors as the underlying cause for elderly subjects' reduced performance (Baltes & Baltes, 1990). Elderly people seem to be more sensitive to variation in task familiarity than younger adults, and the relative complexity of the task is also associated with a reduction in performance. Another frequently reported effect is related to the timing of responses. Elderly people have greater difficulty in tasks in which they are required to produce answers quickly. This effect has been noted by Gaylord and Marsh (1975), who used the paradigm originally developed by Shepard and Metzler (1971) to investigate the effects of mental rotation. Participants were required to judge the similarity of a pair of stimuli by mentally rotating one figure. Although the general effect was confirmed, that is, the time required for the rotation was dependent on the increasing angle between the two figures presented, elderly people needed more time to perform the task and produced more errors. Similar results have been reported in more recent years with tasks substantially similar to those used by Gaylord and Marsh (Dror & Kosslyn, 1994; Hertzog & Rypma, 1991). These studies indicate that one of the critical variables in interpreting the performance of elderly people is the speed of processing. Elderly participants always take longer to perform the tasks but it is interesting to note that when they are not confined by a predetermined time limit, their performance does not differ significantly from younger adults in terms of correctness (Sharps & Gollin, 1987). Further to these studies, the hypothesis that reduced processing speed could be crucial to interpreting cognitive ageing has gained widespread support (Cerella, 1991; Rabbitt, 1981; Salthouse, 1991, 1996; Salthouse & Coon, 1993; Salthouse & Meinz, 1995).

The idea of reduced processing speed has been associated with the assumption that the central components of WM are generally more impaired with increasing age. Among the first to introduce this idea was Welford who, in 1958, hypothesised that ageing produces a limited ability to coordinate and organise information in memory. This idea was not originally related to the WM system but it is clearly consistent with the assumption of selective impairment of central executive structures (Baddeley, 1986). The idea of selective deterioration of specific WM functions was later investigated in more detail, with various materials (verbal and visuo-spatial), and in association with different theoretical assumptions. In 1988, Gick, Craik, and Morris administered verbal tasks to young and older people and found that passive memory load did not affect subjects' performance while an increase in executive functions selectively affected the performance of the elderly (see also Craik & Jennings, 1992). Most studies in this line have proposed visuo-spatial tasks, for example by Salthouse and Mitchell (1989), who suggested that it is possible to distinguish between a structural and an operational capacity in WM functions. Structural capacity refers to the number of information units that can be memorised at the same time, while operational capacity refers to the number of processing operations that can be performed. Two tasks (memorising information and performing operations) were designed to represent measures of structural and operational capacities and the authors confirmed their hypothesis of a selective impairment of operational capacities in elderly people in the absence of significant differences in structural capacity.

In a different theoretical perspective Mayr and Kliegl (1993; Mayr, Kliegl, & Krampe, 1996) suggested that it is necessary to distinguish between sequential and coordination complexity: Pronounced age differences were reported in the most active tasks requiring the integration and coordination of different information. Despite this evidence, data are not so straightforward. In 1991, Salthouse, Babcock, and Shaw tried to replicate their results of 2 years earlier, but found that it was not possible to distinguish the two groups following the dissociation between structural and operational capacities. To test the hypothesis that young and elderly people may be differentiated on the basis of structural and operational capacities, the authors designed an elegant experimental procedure in which participants had to memorise stimuli that appeared on a computer screen and later perform a number of operations on a limited number of stimuli only (Salthouse et al., 1991). These tasks were clearly unfamiliar to elderly participants (in particular the use of the computer, the lack of a connection with everyday life) and the experimental procedure was rather complex. The discrepant data obtained in this study could be the result of the limited tools available to test visuo-spatial abilities, particularly active ones.

INVESTIGATION OF ACTIVE VSWM ABILITIES IN THE ELDERLY: THE JIGSAW PUZZLE TEST

The lack of adequate tools for visuo-spatial assessment, and in particular active visuo-spatial processes, has been a major flaw affecting both experimental practice and clinical or neuropsychological assessment. Various tasks measuring the short-term memory of spatial positions have been developed and used widely (see also Chapter 1). These serve as a common ground for assessing elderly people's passive visuo-spatial abilities in a wide range of situations. However, it is difficult to find procedures to evaluate the manipulation and transformation of visuo-spatial stimuli appropriate for testing the elderly.

A great effort to produce an experimental procedure for measuring active visuo-spatial processing has been made by Vecchi and Richardson (2000; Richardson & Vecchi, 2002). The Jigsaw Puzzle test (JPT) was developed with the aim of producing a task in which the passive load is constantly minimal in the presence of variations in active load, that is, in the amount of information that has to be actively transformed or manipulated. Participants are presented with fragmented pictures of everyday objects taken from the Snodgrass and Vanderwart (1980) standardised set. Pictures are cut into 4, 6, 9, 12, or 16 numbered pieces and the name of the corresponding object is announced aloud as the pieces are presented to the subject (see Figure 1.8, p. 25).

While examining the fragments, participants have a response sheet in front of them consisting of a completely blank grid, divided into the corresponding number of pieces. Subjects have to write down the numbers corresponding to the original fragments in order to solve the jigsaw puzzle. Fragments are always in plain view so the passive load is minimal; at the same time, participants know the name of the object to exclude any object-recognition effect.

Although this test is superficially similar to other procedures used to assess different sorts of visuo-spatial abilities, such as the Puzzle Test for children (see Chapter 4), the Hooper Visual Recognition test (Hooper, 1958), the WAIS Object Assembly subtest (Wechsler, 1981), or the Poltrock and Brown Figure Integration task (1984), it has been designed to have distinctive features. There is no object recognition involved, differing from the Hooper Visual Recognition test, in which the recognition of the object is the main issue of the task. At the same time, knowing the name of the object minimises difficulties in generating the correct image of the picture. Unlike the Poltrock and Brown (1984) procedure, the fragments are not presented one at a time; the pieces are presented together and are always in plain view to minimise the passive memory load. To prevent a perceptual aid in organising the fragments, they do not differ in shape (all are rectangular) and subjects cannot move or join the single pieces. Empirical investigations have confirmed that this task is very sensitive at detecting individual differences in active visuo-spatial abilities, and it is especially helpful in testing elderly subjects (Richardson & Vecchi, 2002; Vecchi & Cornoldi, 1999) or neuropsychological older patients (Vecchi, Saveriano, & Paciaroni, 1998/1999).

Initial data with young adults were encouraging enough to proceed in evaluating the characteristics of the JPT and a second set of experiments was planned to address the possibility of using this task with elderly participants (Richardson & Vecchi, 2002). In these experiments, the JPT was proposed to three groups of participants. Young adults were compared with a group of young elderly (60 to 70 years old) and a group of old elderly (70 to 80 years old). Results indicate that the JPT is highly sensitive in detecting age differences. Differences are always significant among the three groups in terms of both accuracy and time latency. The elderly made more errors and needed more time to perform the task. Moreover, the old elderly group always performed worse than the young elderly group, confirming that the JPT could be used to detect rather small differences according to limited age variations between groups of elderly subjects (Figure 5.1). Richardson and Vecchi (2002) also replicated and enlarged the effect of visual complexity, present in young adults reported in the previous study (Vecchi & Richardson, 2000). Generally, increases in visual complexity produced a reduction in performance, apart from the highest levels which, on the contrary, facilitated individuation of the correct connections.

An investigation of the structures used by the elderly to carry out the JPT confirmed data obtained in the previous study. Once again, Richardson and Vecchi presented the task in a baseline condition and three different

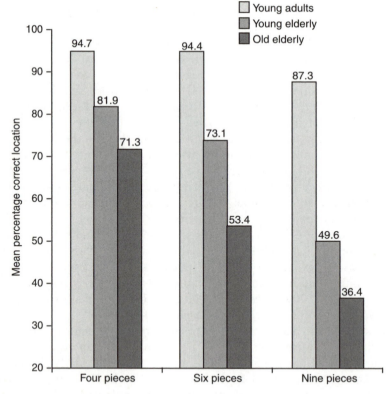

Figure 5.1. Mean percentage correct locations as a function of number of pieces for the young adults, the young elderly, and the old elderly groups (adapted from Richardson & Vecchi, 2002, Exp. 1).

interfering conditions to evaluate the contribution of the various WM components in carrying out the JPT. Interference was visuo-spatial, verbal, and central. Results indicate that young and elderly participants used similar mechanisms in carrying out the task and, while verbal interference was similar to the baseline condition (indicating a very limited contribution of verbal abilities to the JPT), both visuo-spatial and central interference disrupted performance. These data are coherent with the authors' analysis of the task characteristics, specifically visuo-spatial, but also the involvement of more central components of WM.

AGEING EFFECTS AND THE ARCHITECTURE OF VISUO-SPATIAL MEMORY MODELS

The main characteristics of the JPT have been defined in terms of sensitivity, reliability, and flexibility for experimental use. However, two issues remained unexplored: the development of a rapid and easy to administer procedure, and an investigation of the relationship between the JPT and other visuo-spatial tests used in clinical and experimental practice. These two issues are important both from a theoretical perspective (is the JPT really tapping active visuo-spatial processes?) and in addressing practical aspects (can the JPT be adopted routinely to measure visuo-spatial abilities?). Although participants' comments were positive in evaluating the familiarity and ecological value of the JPT, these initial experiments were rather long, with complex procedures to allow the authors to evaluate response criteria (percentage of correct positions or time latencies), characteristics of the pieces (effect of mental rotation), and characteristics of the entire picture (effects of visual complexity). It was necessary to prepare a shorter version of the task facilitating use of the JPT in clinical assessment, and it was decided to design a span version with five increasing levels of complexity. Puzzles could consist of 4, 6, 9, 12, or 16 numbered pieces and the time limit was fixed at 90 s for each picture. The JPT span was incorporated in a battery of eight WM tasks carried our by a sample of 72 young and old participants (Vecchi & Cornoldi, 1999). The investigation was mainly designed to test the hypothesis that elderly WM difficulties concern active components to a greater extent than passive ones. The battery included six tasks, divided into passive and active, which concerned spatial simultaneous, spatial sequential, and visual imagery components of WM. A passive and an active verbal task were used as controls. The distinction between sequential and simultaneous spatial processes was suggested by Pazzaglia and Cornoldi (1999) and we used the Corsi task and Mental Pathway task (passive and active, respectively) as examples of the former category, and for the latter the Visual Pattern test (Della Sala et al., 1997) and a variation of this test in which the response matrices were rotated (passive and active). Visual imagery abilities were evaluated through memory of a coloured configuration task and the JPT. As verbal tasks, a verbal span and an Italian version of Daneman and Carpenter's (1980) Listening Span task adapted by De Beni et al. (1998) were used (passive and active, respectively). A principal component analysis yielded three factors that fit exactly with our predictions. The first factor is active (but these and other data suggest that it could be differentiated further), and factors 2 and 3 were clearly related to the visuo-spatial and verbal passive tasks (Vecchi & Cornoldi, 1999).

The JPT was confirmed as a measure of active visuo-spatial processes and at the same time provided the first indications about the structure of WM processes following process-dependent and information-dependent perspectives (Vecchi & Cornoldi, 1999). Active tasks tend to group together, although loading is lower for the verbal active tasks. On the contrary, passive tasks tend to be differentiated on the basis of the characteristics being processed, namely verbal or visuo-spatial, with the exception of the Corsi task, which presented a peculiar pattern (see also Vecchi & Richardson, 2001). Distance between tasks is a function of both variables and although a degree of modality-specific processes are present at all levels, the extent to which the processes are dissociated decreases as a function of increasing active load.

These data have been replicated in a further investigation with a larger sample of subjects (204 participants ranging from 19 to 70 years old) and the administration of six tasks (Richardson & Vecchi, 2002, Exp. 4). The verbal span and the Italian version of the Listening Span task were again used to test passive and active verbal abilities, and the Corsi task, the Visual Pattern test, the Mental Pathway task, and the JPT span were used as measures of passive and active visuo-spatial processes. Results were very straightforward: Three factors were identified in a factorial analysis. The first was related to verbal processes (verbal span and Listening Span task), the second to active visuo-spatial processing (JPT and Mental Pathway test), and the third to passive visuo-spatial processes (Corsi and Visual Pattern tests) (Richardson & Vecchi, 2002).

In this case, it was confirmed that the JPT should be considered a measure of active visuo-spatial processes, but it should also be highlighted that modality-specific effects may be present at higher levels of processing. Moreover, the JPT obtained higher loadings than the Mental Pathway task, suggesting that it could be considered a purer measure of active visuo-spatial processing. To investigate this issue further, a direct comparison of these two measures of active visuo-spatial processes was carried out and confirmed that both tests are reliable measures of active visuo-spatial processes but that the JPT is significantly more sensitive to age differences than the Mental Pathway task (Bosco, Cavallini, Longoni, Richardson, & Vecchi, 2002).

PROCESS-DEPENDENT EFFECTS IN OLD AGE

Development of these tools to assess active visuo-spatial processes makes it possible to disentangle the discrepancies that emerged from the studies of Salthouse and colleagues (Salthouse et al., 1991; Salthouse & Mitchell, 1989) of the structural vs. operational visuo-spatial capacity decay in the elderly. We addressed this issue from a passive vs. active processes perspective in the study mentioned in the preceding paragraph, using six different visuo-spatial tasks—three passive and three active—with a sample of three groups divided by age (Vecchi & Cornoldi, 1999). Young adults were compared with groups of young elderly and old elderly (60 to 70 and 70 to 80 years old, respectively). The mean performances of the three groups for the six tasks are reported in Table 5.1.

Analyses were performed on the six different tasks and indicated that all tasks (with the exception of the Corsi task) showed an age-related effect. However, significant differences between the two groups of elderly were reported for the active tasks only. This result supports the data obtained by Salthouse and Mitchell (1989), indicating that elderly people have selective problems in manipulating and transforming visuo-spatial information. Conversely, active tasks are very sensitive tools for investigating memory performance in old age and, more generally, cognitive ageing.

To confirm and enlarge data on the importance of investigating individual differences in visuo-spatial abilities through measures of active manipulation, Vecchi and colleagues (1998/1999) compared a group of demented patients with a control group of normal aged subjects. The importance of central executive components in Alzheimer-type dementia has been confirmed repeatedly (see Baddeley, Bressi, Della Sala, Logie, & Spinnler, 1991; Baddeley, Logie, Bressi, Della Sala, & Spinnler, 1986; Morris, 1996) and it was reasonable to hypothesise a selective decay in active tasks in the pathological

Table 5.1
Mean span scores in the six visuo-spatial tasks as a function of age (adapted from Vecchi & Cornoldi, 1999). Reprinted with permission.

	Young adults	Young elderly	Old elderly
Passive tasks			
Spatial simultaneous	7.15	5.37	4.74
Spatial sequential	5.52	5.22	5.13
Visual imagery	6.68	4.54	3.87
Active tasks			
Spatial simultaneous	4.65	3.23	2.01
Spatial sequential	9.81	6.72	4.54
Visual imagery	8.41	5.20	2.66

group. Four tasks were presented, two passive (Corsi blocks and verbal span) and two active (Mental Pathway task and Nonword Generation task—in which participants put together the initial letters of syllables presented in sequence to generate the resulting nonword). It is clear from Table 5.2 that demented patients performed significantly worse than the elderly group in all tasks. However, the difference was significantly higher for active tasks, in which a dramatic drop in performance is reported: The deficit is maximised in both the Mental Pathway and Nonword Generation tasks.

Overall, results confirm the importance of dissociating passive and active visuo-spatial processes but leave an open question that could, in principle, apply to all studies addressing the passive/active distinction, and which is particularly important in the case of the elderly. If the active tasks are simply more complex (and therefore more difficult) than their passive siblings, it is possible that reduced general ability associated with ageing (in terms of cognitive resources or general WM capacity) influences the active tasks to a greater extent, with a minor effect on the easier passive tasks. This point has been a major flaw in most studies on cognitive ageing. To disentangle this issue it is necessary not only to compare performance in passive and active tasks but also to find a passive task that is more difficult than its active counterpart. A modification of the JPT paradigm addresses this point. In this version, the JPT incorporates both a passive and an active task in a single experimental trial (Vecchi, Richardson, & Cavallini, 2002). Participants are first required to solve the puzzle by reorganising the pieces (as described above). Immediately after this, they are presented with a blank matrix only, representing the initial positions of the pieces, which they then have to place (they have the actual pieces in their hands) in the original jumbled configuration. This procedure (Vecchi et al., 2002) allowed the performances in the passive and active tasks to be matched directly, since the initial stimuli and scoring procedures (number of pieces in the correct positions) are

Table 5.2

Mean span scores in the four memory tasks as a function of material (verbal vs. visuo-spatial, process (passive vs. active), and age (adapted from Vecchi et al., 1998/1999).

	Elderly	*Alzheimer*	*Effect size*
Passive tasks			
Verbal	4.16	3.34	1.04
Visuo-spatial	4.18	3.43	0.71
Active tasks			
Verbal	3.93	1.04	1.82
Visuo-spatial	5.10	0.81	1.46

Measures of effect size are calculated following Cohen's method (Cohen, 1969) as reported in Richardson (1996).

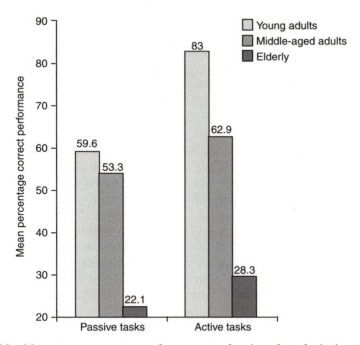

Figure 5.2.   Mean percentage correct performance as a function of age for both passive and active tasks (from Vecchi et al., 2002, Exp. 2).

the same in both cases. The results show that the passive task is more difficult than the active. It therefore appears to be the ideal procedure for investigating the interaction of processing and complexity effects in VSWM. The three groups—young adults, middle-aged adults, and elderly—were presented with trials consisting of pictures fragmented in four, six, or nine pieces and performances are reported in Figure 5.2.

Results confirm that ageing effects are more evident in active rather than passive tasks, and this is independent of task difficulty. Moreover, the data offer the possibility of examining the specific effects of number of pieces (a variable that can be considered as affecting complexity). Results show that variations in the number of pieces have a greater effect on the passive task than the active, confirming that degree of activity and complexity can be distinguished.

CONCLUDING REMARKS

Altogether, these data strongly support previous studies on passive and active capacities in all kinds of individual difference paradigms. Distinctions between passive and active abilities in visuo-spatial processes are extremely relevant in explaining cognitive ageing as well as other related individual differences, including deficits originating from pathological conditions such as Alzheimer-type dementia. The limitations of the elderly in visuo-spatial abilities are significantly more evident in tasks requiring information to be manipulated and transformed. This result should not be confused with a generalised complexity effect. Active tasks are selectively compromised in old age, even if the material is designed to have simpler procedures and higher performances. Other studies have also indicated that ageing effects in cognitive tasks cannot be confused or otherwise masked by experience factors or strategic capacities. Ageing and experience both affect performance but they do not interact with each other, indicating independent effects. From a theoretical perspective, these studies on cognitive ageing provide important data for postulating the VSWM architecture. They also suggest the relationship between the different components of the WM system as a whole, indicating that both process-dependent and information-dependent dimensions should be considered, and suggesting an interaction between these separate aspects.

These data do dot allow us to disentangle the issue of discriminating between the hypotheses of interpreting cognitive ageing as: (1) a product of a unique underlying cause (e.g., processing speed or frontal/executive functions); or (2) a collection of single independent effects. However, WM functions were confirmed to be crucial in interpreting the age-related decay: In particular, the ability to manipulate and integrate information seems to be significantly affected in old age. Moreover, data obtained with visuo-spatial tasks, in contrast with verbal material, often showed significant discrepancies between young and elderly individuals, suggesting that these abilities may be selectively compromised in old age.

CHAPTER SIX

Imagery, blindness, and visuo-spatial working memory

Investigating mental imagery processes in the congenitally blind leads to an understanding of the role of visual perception in generating and manipulating visuo-spatial images and, at the same time, an understanding of the specific characteristics of visuo-spatial mechanisms developed in the absence of visual stimuli. We have already acknowledged that mental images cannot be considered as simply associated to visual or sensorial traces, although different representations can be associated with visuo-spatial, verbal, or haptic information. However, greater sources of perceptual as well as conceptual information may be used, and then integrated to generate and process mental representations (Cornoldi et al., 1998; Cornoldi & Vecchi, 2000). In general terms, it can be assumed that imagery processes do not necessarily depend directly on any sensory modality, and are more complex and heterogeneous cognitive functions.

IMAGERY PROCESSING IN BLIND PEOPLE

At a superficial level it is usually possible to consider the analogies between visual traces and mental images as an indication of equivalence, although the similarities are still unclear. It is therefore particularly important to evaluate imagery abilities in the congenitally blind, and to isolate the role of visual perception. In fact, several studies have now established that the congenitally blind are able to form and manipulate mental images, using either perceptual information (verbal or haptic) or long-term knowledge. Zimler and Keenan

(1983) reported that the performance of sighted and congenitally blind people in tasks requiring mental imagery was very similar. This result has also been confirmed by Kerr (1983), but she added that the generation process could be significantly slower in the blind. These data confirm that blind people's images are qualitatively similar to those of sighted people, and typical features are present in both cases. Further support comes from Marmor and Zaback's (1976) study, which reported that mechanisms underlying mental rotation do exist in the congenitally blind and work in a similar fashion, and from the investigation carried out by Jonides, Kahn, and Rozin (1975) indicating that the memory performance of the blind improves when an imagery strategy is used. The result reported by Marmor (1978) is especially provocative, showing that congenital blindness does not preclude the mental representation of colours.

Marmor and Zaback (1976) used the traditional Shepard and Metzler paradigm to evaluate mental rotation abilities, and Carpenter and Eisemberg (1978) confirmed blind people's ability to rotate mental representation using verbal material such as single letters variously oriented. These authors also noted longer latencies in the blind group associated with a higher number of errors. These data, which suggest an impairment in rotating mental images associated with congenital blindness, are partially confuted by the results obtained by Heller, Calcaterra, Green, and Lima (1999) showing that experience can greatly influence the results. The nonsighted performed better than the sighted in mental rotation tasks when using reversed Braille as stimuli.

In general, the sighted and nonsighted show similar abilities in generating pictures by means of haptic stimuli (Carreiras & Codina, 1992; Kerr, 1983; Klatzky, Golledge, Loomis, Cicinelli, & Pellegrino, 1995) and, altogether, the data reported above confirm that the blind are capable of generating and processing mental images. They also meet specific difficulties and limitations. The nonsighted experience significant difficulty in representing the rules of perspective in mental representations (Arditi, Holtzman, & Kosslyn, 1988) and, similarly, they show limitations in foreshortening drawings (Heller, Calcaterra, Tyler, & Burson, 1996), although drawing abilities are usually preserved (Kennedy, 1982, 1993).

Spatial orientation abilities are usually spared in the congenitally blind, who are able to generate spatial maps and use them to orient themselves in the environment (Loomis, Klatzky, Golledge, Cicinelli, & Pellegrino, 1993). However, other studies have indicated that performance is frequently lower than for the sighted (Reiser, Hill, Talor, Bradfield, & Rosen, 1992). Difficulties are maximised when the nonsighted are required to continuously update mental representations (Reiser, Guth, & Hill, 1986) or evaluate distances and inclinations (Juurmaa & Lehtinen-Railo, 1994).

Congenital blindness does not seem to preclude the ability to generate and process visuo-spatial images, although limitations are frequently reported, often associated with more complex or time-pressured tasks. Both structural and strategic factors have been proposed to explain these differences. Stuart (1995) suggested that the limitations of the nonsighted reflect underlying brain damage while Thinus-Blanc and Gaunet (1997) hypothesised a lack of appropriate strategies. In the remaining part of this chapter we will review some of the studies we have carried out in the last 20 years to evaluate the abilities and limitations of the nonsighted in the use of mental images and we will interpret these data in a WM framework. These studies were mainly carried out with adult individuals of normal intelligence but a complete sensory deficit; blindness was total (no residual visual perception) and congenital (loss of vision from birth).

IMAGERY AND MEMORY EFFECTS IN BLIND PEOPLE

The positive effects of imagery value and imagery strategies in memory tasks has been documented widely (Paivio, 1971). It is interesting to evaluate these effects in a population of congenitally blind people to verify the presence and magnitude of memory improvement associated with higher visual imagery value stimuli in the absence of visual perception. First, it is important to compare the imagery ratings of sighted and nonsighted populations, and then to investigate memory effects in both groups. More than 20 years ago, we investigated these aspects in a study comparing the recall of words grouped in three categories: high-imagery words that can be experienced haptically (HIE), high-imagery words that cannot be perceived haptically and are therefore unavailable to the blind (HINE), and low-imagery words (LI) (Cornoldi, Calore, & Pra Baldi, 1979). Words in the HINE category include *tiger* and *palm-tree*; these nouns have a high imagery value but cannot be experienced by touch. This contrasts with words in the HIE category such as *stone* or *cat*. These categories were compared with LI words, such as *firm* or *pause*, in a recall task. Results showed that the nonsighted were reliable in attributing imagery values to the different words, and that for HINE words their scores were significantly lower. This result is coherent with the fact that these nouns are not perceived directly and so affect imagery ratings. The nonsighted gave higher imagery ratings to LI than to HINE words and this was associated with a high performance in the recall of LI words. However, they recalled the HIE words particularly well. Sighted and nonsighted subjects gave different ratings and, consequently, performed differently, which can be associated with the imagery values of the two groups. Data then confirmed that the nonsighted memory is affected by the stimulus imagery value, although the absence of vision can itself produce different imagery ratings and a different pattern of performance. Apart from the difference between the two groups regarding the HINE words (which we have also recently replicated; Tinti, Galati, Vecchio, De Beni, & Cornoldi, 1999), nonsighted subjects scored higher than sighted in incidental and intentional recall tasks with LI words. This result suggests that blindness could lead to different imagery effects, possibly integrated with alternative and more efficient strategies, which are not necessarily verbal, as we were also able to find imagery effects after excluding the use of verbal strategies by the nonsighted (Vecchi, 1998).

To improve our understanding of imagery effects in the nonsighted, we chose to analyse the effects of imagery mnemonics in the congenitally blind (De Beni & Cornoldi, 1985a, 1985b). Blindness does not generally preclude the beneficial effect of imagery strategies. In this case the strategy used was the Loci Mnemonic associated with recalling a list of 20 words. The nonsighted demonstrated that they were using an imagery strategy, which led to an improved performance. However, we also found specific limitations in the nonsighted group: When an experimental manipulation required a nonsighted subject to generate and use complex interactive images, a selective difficulty was found (De Beni & Cornoldi, 1985a). Sighted subjects were successful if required to generate multiple images, whereas nonsighted subjects reported a major difficulty. This is the first study in which we pinpointed that blindness, although not precluding the ability to generate and use mental images, produces specific memory limitations. This result has recently been replicated (Tinti et al., 1999), also indicating that the facilitating effect due to multiple images could appear in blind individuals in specific conditions, such as multiple auditory images. This confirms that mental images, although not directly dependent on a specific sensory input, have modality-specific features. This conclusion is further supported by a study of Aleman, Van Lee, Mantione, Verkoijen, and De Haan (2001) who showed that congenitally totally blind people were able to perform tasks that are mediated by visual mental imagery in sighted people, but also that they were affected by interference from a concurrent tapping task to the same extent as control subjects with normal vision.

The effect of the overall complexity of the image to be generated, selectively affecting blind people's performance, has been confirmed by a subsequent study in which pairs and triplets of words had to be organised in an interactive image (De Beni & Cornoldi, 1988). Multiple images have always been associated with low performance in the congenitally blind and we confirmed that specific limitations are found when manipulating the characteristics of the mental representation. Similar data have indicated that congenital blindness affects the possibility of linking images sequentially (Cornoldi & De Beni, 1988). We also tested the possibility that specific characteristics of the material could affect blind people's images and we studied the bizarre imagery effect (McDaniel & Einstein, 1986) to verify whether the inclusion of rare and bizarre pictures could result in the same facilitation for sighted and nonsighted groups (Cornoldi, De Beni, Roncari, & Romano, 1989). The performances of the two groups were comparable. Moreover, we also replicated the selective difficulty for nonsighted populations of generating interactive images that include more than one item at the same time. However, the specific nature of this deficit was still unclear and a line of research focused on this issue was then developed, by linking imagery limitations to the capacity of the cognitive structure hypothesised to underlie mental imagery—WM and VSWM in particular.

VISUO-SPATIAL WORKING MEMORY LIMITATIONS IN CONGENITAL BLINDNESS

In Chapter 2 we described a methodology that we have used repeatedly to investigate VSWM processes in humans: passive matrices and active pathway tasks. These tasks originated from the studies of Attneave and Curlee (1983) and Kerr (1987), who first developed an experimental procedure requiring participants to move sequentially through matrices of various dimensions and follow a pathway for a series of statements of direction. We decided to use this task to investigate passive and active VSWM processes in the nonsighted, and adapted the procedure for use in a haptic modality. Printed matrices were substituted with wooden cubes arranged in different ways to form matrices of various sizes. Patterns could then be easily explored by touch, and nonsighted subjects could indicate the final position of the pathway in the wooden matrices. Similarly, passive tasks were prepared by including a number of sandpaper-covered wooden cubes, which were easily identifiable in a haptic exploration of the pattern. Participants could then recognise target positions, and later point to those cubes in an entirely blank matrix. These tasks address both theoretical and methodological issues. Passive and active processes can be explored in comparable conditions and the experimental procedures are identical for the blindfolded sighted and nonsighted participants. Experimental manipulation was identical to that described in previous chapters in the investigation of passive and active VSWM processes. Passive tasks could consist of different-sized matrices, including a varying number of target positions, and pathways were identified by means of a series of statements of direction (forwards–backwards, left–right, and up–down in the case of 3D matrices only).

The first study investigating VSWM capacity in the nonsighted using the tactual matrix procedures was undertaken with the explicit aim of comparing processing limitations in sighted and nonsighted subjects (Cornoldi et al., 1991b). We prepared 2D and 3D matrices, which were comparable for either the number of cubes (3 × 3 vs. 2 × 2 × 2, or 8 × 8 vs. 4 × 4 × 4 matrices) or number of cubes in each dimension (3 × 3 vs. 3 × 3 × 3, or 4 × 4 vs. 4 × 4 × 4 matrices). These conditions were used to verify the hypothesis put forward by

Kerr (1987), who suggested that the number of cubes in each dimension, regardless of the overall size of the matrix, influences performance. In particular, mental imagery capacity should be fixed as a function of maximum number of elements per side. Kerr indicated a limit of three elements per side, regardless of the number of sides (dimensions), that is, 9 cubes in a 2D pattern and 27 cubes in a 3D pattern. This hypothesis is rather counterintuitive because it has been shown repeatedly that the overall complexity of the image to be generated is a variable with a great influence on modulating performance in visuo-spatial tasks, particularly in the case of the congenitally blind, as we have already described. In addition, 3D matrices should represent greater difficulty for the nonsighted, given the limitations in generating multiple or interactive images produced by congenital blindness. The first experiments we carried out (Cornoldi et al., 1991b) consisted of the execution of active pathways only, and the results confirm that blind people may successfully use visuo-spatial mental imagery, but they present specific limitations. Three-dimensional matrices are more difficult for the nonsighted than the corresponding 2D ones, or even 2D matrices including a higher number of cubes.

In this research, we used the Pathway task only, with sequences including seven statements of direction. The effect of dimension (2D vs. 3D) is evident and in contrast with the data obtained by Kerr in 1987. Kerr herself, in 1993, published a study showing that her results with 3D patterns were due to a particularly high level of visuo-spatial ability. We also investigated the possible role of verbal mediation in carrying out the Pathway task, and the possible difference between sighted and nonsighted groups. Although a verbal strategy could be used in specific conditions, results show that the sighted and nonsighted adopted it to a similar extent. The issue of the use of a verbal strategy in carrying out visuo-spatial tasks has also been investigated in further research. Recently, we proposed both spatial position and mental pathway tasks in a baseline condition, as well as in association with an articulatory suppression interfering task. Results once again indicate that in this task neither group uses a verbal strategy or, if they do, all subjects use it to a similar extent (Figure 6.1).

It is therefore clear that the nonsighted are able to use specific visuo-spatial processes. When the task, especially an active task, becomes too difficult, a verbal strategy may be used to improve performance by sighted and nonsighted subjects (Cornoldi et al., 1991b). However, as we expected, 3D matrices proved to be particularly difficult for the nonsighted to generate and process, and this result needed to be understood.

In 1993, we again compared 2D and 3D matrices with comparable numbers of squares (3×3 and 5×5 vs. $2 \times 2 \times 2$ and $3 \times 3 \times 3$) for two reasons: since (1) this level of complexity seemed to be more sensitive in identifying individual differences associated with congenital blindness; and (2) this

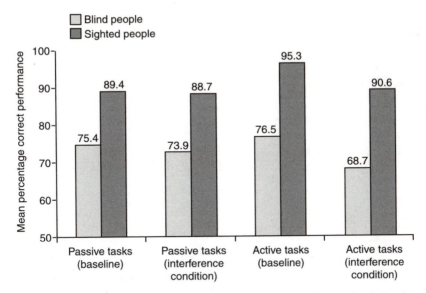

Figure 6.1. Mean percentage correct performance as a function of type of task (passive vs. active) and interference conditions (with or without articulatory suppression) for blind and sighted participants (adapted from Vecchi, 1998).

variable, in contrast to Kerr's hypothesis, turned out to be associated with VSWM capacity (Cornoldi, Bertuccelli, Rocchi, & Sbrana, 1993). Once again, the Pathway task was adopted and, in addition, we introduced a further experimental manipulation—the presentation rate associated with the sequence of statements of direction. A slow presentation rate of one statement every 2 s was compared with a fast condition in which statements were read in 1 s. Although congenital blindness always determined a significantly lower performance, presentation rate affected both groups to a similar extent. The 2 s rate was the ideal condition in the Pathway task but, again, the nonsighted showed selective impairment in the case of 3D patterns.

ACTIVE AND PASSIVE VISUO-SPATIAL PROCESSES IN BLIND PEOPLE

Data were therefore consistent in indicating a decrement in performance by the nonsighted associated with specific task demands, namely the need to generate complex interacting or multiple images and the presence of 3D patterns. It is possible that similar limitations are responsible for both effects. In 1995, we tested the hypothesis that blindness-related difficulties were related to the difference between passive and active VSWM processes (Vecchi et al., 1995). Again, using a wooden matrix to compare sighted and nonsighted performances, we proposed both the passive (spatial positions) and

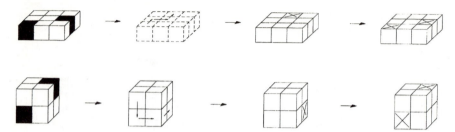

Figure 6.2. Examples of the sequential procedures involving both passive and active tasks (see Figure 3.1). Target cubes were differentiated by covering them with sandpaper to allow them to be easily recognised by touch.

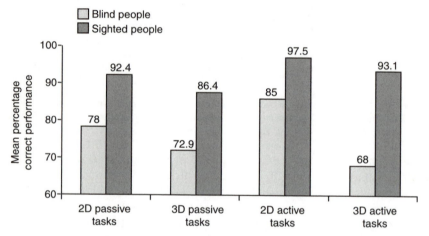

Figure 6.3. Mean percentage correct performance as a function of type of task (passive vs. active) and number of dimensions (2D vs. 3D) for blind and sighted participants (adapted from Vecchi, 1998).

active (mental pathway) tasks in the same experimental session, following the procedure described in Chapter 3. Subjects were initially required to touch the wooden matrix to identify the target squares, then to follow the sequence of statements of direction. Participants were finally presented with a completely neutral wooden matrix and asked to point to the final position of the pathway and to the positions previously occupied by the target cubes. In the first study, we used a 5 × 5 matrix with active tasks consisting of eight movements and passive positions including either two or five cubes. Results clearly indicate that the two groups' performances do not differ for passive tasks, whereas nonsighted subjects show a significant reduction in the active tasks.

In a following study (Vecchi, 1998), to increase performance level and evaluate more precisely the difference between sighted and nonsighted subjects in both passive and active tasks, we decided to use simpler 2D and 3D matrices. We compared 3 × 3 and 2 × 2 × 2 matrices in the dual-task procedure described above, including both a memory for position and pathway tasks (Figure 6.2).

Although performances of the nonsighted were lower in all conditions, differences were greater with 3D matrices and maximised in the active tasks (Figure 6.3).

BLINDNESS AND THE USE OF THE THIRD DIMENSION

Our series of studies consistently demonstrates an evident effect due to type of task (passive vs. active) and, at the same time, a difficulty associated with the use of the third dimension. The 3D effect is stable across conditions and experiments but we still need to understand the underlying reason *why* 3D patterns create greater difficulty for the congenitally blind. It is possible that a 3D representation could include more than one "picture," implying the concurrent maintenance and processing of more than one image. This should produce an impairment associated with difficulty in processing multiple or interacting images. We therefore carried out a new series of experiments (Cornoldi, Tinti, & Vecchi, 2002b) seeking to understanding the specific deficit associated with the third dimension in the congenitally blind.

The first experiment was designed to investigate whether the congenitally blind are impaired in passive recall tasks requiring the generation of multiple images. We compared the recall of an equal number of positions presented within either a single 5 × 5 matrix or divided in two 5 × 5 matrices (Figure 6.4).

Although the two-matrices condition was more difficult for all subjects, we found a significant interaction between number of matrices and group, indicating that the congenitally blind have selective problems remembering two matrices at the same time (Figure 6.5).

The limitations of the nonsighted in tasks requiring the generation of

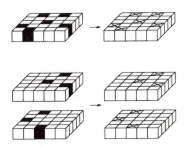

Figure 6.4. Examples of trials comprising the memorisation and recall of single (top) vs. multiple (bottom) matrices comprising the same number of targets.

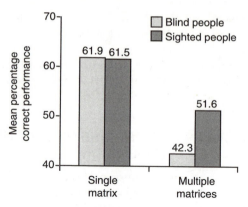

Figure 6.5.   Mean percentage correct performance as a function of number of matrices for blind and sighted participants (from Cornoldi et al., 2002b).

multiple images have been confirmed repeatedly, as acknowledged above. However, no studies have so far addressed the difference between generating multiple images and the need to integrate the information present in two or more images. The problem shown by blind people in the previous experiment highlights the difficulty of generating more than one image at a time, and possibly an inability to shift continuously from one image to another to refresh all the information. However, it is possible that the nonsighted also have difficulty integrating all the information. To disentangle this issue we compared two conditions; one in which sighted and nonsighted subjects had to memorise and remember two separate matrices presented together, and the other in which the initial stimuli were presented in two separate matrices but the response matrix was unique and participants were required to generate an image comprising targets presented in both initial stimuli, thus integrating the different information (Figure 6.6).

The interaction between response condition (multiple images vs. integration condition) and group was significant, indicating that congenitally blind people have difficulty representing more than one image at a time but not in integrating information from different external stimuli. The performances of the two groups were comparable in the integration condition, where answers had to be provided in a unique matrix. However, differences were again evident in the multiple image condition, in which the initial material was coincident with the response matrices (Figure 6.7).

Sighted subjects were not substantially affected by the request to integrate the different items of information, and this also facilitated the nonsighted group, perhaps by reducing the information to be remembered. Multiple images were associated with the deficit observed for the nonsighted.

Blind people's difficulty in treating 3D visuo-spatial patterns seems a

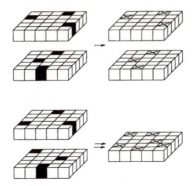

Figure 6.6. Examples of trials comprising the memorisation and recall of multiple matrices (top) or the integration of the targets in a single response matrix (bottom).

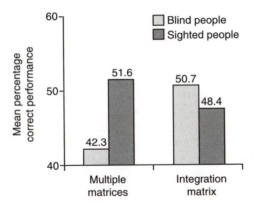

Figure 6.7. Mean percentage correct performance as a function of response matrices (two matrices/multiple vs. single matrix/integration) for blind and sighted participants (from Cornoldi et al., 2002b).

puzzling, complex phenomenon influenced by a number of different variables. Our provisional results suggest that the request to maintain several elements simultaneously may be more critical than the request to integrate these elements. However, other variables may contribute to determining the 3D difficulty. In particular, to complete our understanding of the variables affecting 3D processing in nonsighted subjects, we evaluated the role of the vertical dimension by designing an active pathway task in which a 4 × 4 matrix was presented in the vertical orientation, and statements of direction were up–down and right–left only. This condition was contrasted with the task using the traditional horizontal matrix comprising forwards–backwards and right–left movements as instructions. As in the previous experiments, a sample of congenitally blind subjects was tested and matched with a control

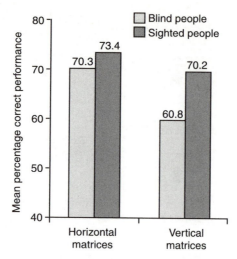

Figure 6.8.   Mean percentage correct performance as a function of the orientation of the stimulus matrix (horizontal vs. vertical) for blind and sighted participants (from Cornoldi et al., 2002b).

group of sighted individuals. The data indicate that 3D difficulties may also be associated with using the vertical dimension.

Figure 6.8 shows that differences between the two groups are not significant regarding horizontal matrices. At the same time, for sighted subjects there is no difference between following pathways in horizontal or vertical matrices. On the contrary, there is a pronounced reduction in the performance of nonsighted subjects for vertical matrices, thus producing a significant difference between the two groups in this condition only.

CONCLUDING REMARKS

The results reported in this chapter indicate that the nonsighted are able to generate and process mental images within the VSWM system. At the same time, research has also highlighted specific limitations that may be due to the absence of sight. Studies with congenitally blind individuals are especially relevant in helping us understand the role of visual perception in the generation and manipulation of visuo-spatial images. We have repeatedly emphasised that the absence of vision does not impede an efficient visuo-spatial system functioning. These effects could be due to the support of other sensory modalities; in particular, the similarities between vision and haptic modalities have also been reported often (Easton, Srinivas, & Greene, 1997). However, characteristics of the system are likely to be different, sometimes leading to selective difficulties and limitations. These limitations could be overcome if information is encoded within a modality other than vision (Tinti et al., 1999), suggesting that mental images maintain modality-specific features.

Blind people's VSWM presents selective deficits in active processing abilities. We have now seen that these data are frequent in research into individual differences. However, we also have sufficient information to suggest that not all deficits are the same and that similar outcomes could be the result of very different processes. In Chapter 4, we saw that gender- and blindness-related effects are independent. A different use of strategies could be involved in the former case, and structural differences in the case of the nonsighted. This does not exclude the possibility that strategies could also affect the performance of the nonsighted, as suggested by Thinus-Blanc and Gaunet (1997). However, in our view, differences in the systems' organisation, such as the need to process information sequentially and difficulty in processing information simultaneously, is more likely to produce the limitations observed. In particular, the difficulty of generating and maintaining more than one image at a time is a clear index of simultaneous processing limitations. Other effects, such as difficulty in representing the vertical dimension, are less important for the comprehension of the characteristics of VSWM, although they could help in understanding the limitations associated with congenital blindness in everyday life and should be considered carefully when preparing rehabilitation or re-education programmes.

Active processes may not be associated only to different structures or adopted strategies. Studies with congenitally blind individuals have helped us to disentangle the issue of the different variables influencing the amount of active processing required and have also helped us to identify experimentally the effects of this variable on performance. In our view, first, the complex pattern of results we have obtained testing verbal memory and spatial recall cannot be explained on the basis of a single mechanism. In fact, the lack of visual experience may produce a poorer ability to generate a mental image and memorise specific stimuli. Second, it may also have determined a processing limitation with single spatial configurations only under specific conditions—3D patterns or active operations. Third, blind people's VSWM difficulty seems to be related to the request to generate, maintain, and manipulate more than one image at a time.

CHAPTER SEVEN

Visuo-spatial abilities in genetic syndromes

The effect of genetic syndromes on cognitive ability was widely investigated during the 1990s. Cognitive patterns connected with gene mutations have generally been associated with conditions of mental retardation. However, this classification is now considered an over-simplification since: (1) several studies have demonstrated that the different conditions produce different intellectual levels; and (2) similar general intelligence scores can also present typical cognitive patterns. There are evident differences between Down and Williams syndromes, as well as between Turner syndrome and Fragile-X mutations. In particular, a peculiar pattern of visuo-spatial abilities has been highlighted in the different pathologies and often investigated in a direct comparison, for example, between Down and Williams syndromes. In the following paragraphs we will analyse visuo-spatial functions in the different populations from neurobiological, neuropsychological, and behavioural perspectives.

DOWN'S SYNDROME

Down's syndrome (DS) was classified by John Down who, in the mid-nineteenth century, described a clinical condition characterised by marked physical features (large lips, narrow palpebral fissure, oblique eyes, thick tongue) and mental retardation (Down, 1866, 1887). This genetic disorder can be identified in a triplication of chromosome 21. In the most frequent condition, trisomy 21, the disorder is associated with a dysfunction in the first meiotic division, although forms of translocation—the additional chromosome is linked to another chromosome—and mosaicism are also present (Carter, 1979; Cooper & Hall, 1988). Several morphological brain differences are often associated with DS: typical shape and different pattern of convolutions, incomplete development of the frontal areas, and hypoplasia. Several studies have also indicated that the cognitive pattern emerging in DS does not coincide with other forms of mental retardation (Vicari, Albertini, & Caltagirone, 1992; Wang, Doherty, Rourke & Bellugi, 1995) or with the cognitive decline associated with normal or pathological ageing (Caltagirone, Nocentini, & Vicari, 1990; Vicari, Nocentini, & Caltagirone, 1994).

To be able to investigate visuo-spatial abilities in DS, it is extremely important to analyse possible neuroanatomical differences in the areas that play a greater role in spatial processes, such as the hippocampus. Since O'Keefe and Nadel's review in 1978, several authors have shown the importance of the hippocampus in spatial cognition and it has been demonstrated that the hippocampus of DS individuals is often smaller (Jernigan, Bellugi, Sowell, Doherty, & Hesselink, 1993), with a reduced number of nerve cells (Ball & Nuttal, 1981) associated to dendritic anomalies (Ferrer & Gullotta, 1990). On these grounds, Uecker, Mangan, Obrzut, and Nadel (1993) undertook an investigation to further understand the neurobiological correlates of DS and effects on spatial abilities. Uecker and colleagues considered the available experimental evidence, investigating place learning, spatial localisation, and visuo-spatial functions in DS. They concluded that a selective deficit in spatial representation abilities could underlie a knowledge acquisition deficit in all domains, thus producing the general mental retardation pattern observed in DS. Children with DS had a selective difficulty in a spatial learning task (Uecker et al., 1993) and young DS individuals were selectively impaired in a spatial relocation task (Katz & Ellis, 1991).

Individuals with DS had pronounced difficulty representing the details of a picture, although they were flawless in tasks requiring them to reproduce the global outline of the picture (Bellugi, Bihrle, Jernigan, Trauner, & Doherty, 1990; Bihrle, Bellugi, Delis, & Marks, 1989). This performance pattern is similar to that of left-hemisphere patients. In fact, it has also been suggested that DS produces more visible deficits in the verbal domain (Fabbretti, Pizzuto, Vicari, & Volterra, 1997), with specific morphosyntactic difficulties in some aspects of verbal comprehension and production (Vicari, Caselli, & Tonucci, 2000a). The nature of visuo-spatial deficits in DS is still rather unclear and it is particularly intriguing that DS individuals do not seem to use analogical strategies in mental rotation. The characteristic pattern of performance, showing that rotation time is related to the angle between the two stimuli, was not always replicated in DS groups, who were more heterogeneous in their pattern of responses (Uecker, Obrzut, & Nadel,

1994). The greatest angles of rotation also facilitated the DS group, whose performance in these conditions was similar to controls.

Overall, the pattern of results is unclear. On the one hand, Uecker and colleagues (Uecker et al., 1993) confirmed that DS individuals experience a marked deficit in at least some aspects of visuo-spatial abilities. On the other hand, a typical left-hemisphere damage pattern is present and a clear verbal deficit is also highlighted. This nonverbal preference is also suggested by the results of a study addressing the relationship between developmental stages of verbal and gesture productions. DS individuals showed a "gesture advantage," again suggesting an earlier development of nonverbal skills (Caselli, Vicari, Longobardi, Lami, Pizzoli, & Stella, 1998). More recent research carried out by Vicari and colleagues (Carlesimo, Marotta, & Vicari, 1996; Fabbretti et al., 1997; Vicari, Bellucci, & Carlesimo, 2000b; Vicari, Carlesimo, & Caltagirone, 1995) has contributed to clarifying the cognitive profiles associated with DS, with specific attention to short- and long-term memory processes in both verbal and visuo-spatial domains.

On the basis of the results reviewed by Hulme and Mackenzie (1992) regarding impairment of the WM system in people with learning disabilities, Vicari and colleagues (1995) hypothesised the possibility of matching verbal and visuo-spatial impairments in DS individuals, at the same time evaluating the role of more central executive functions. Hulme and Mackenzie specifically found a reduction in verbal spans associated with DS, and Vicari and collaborators used both verbal and visuo-spatial spans, in forwards and backwards conditions. DS individuals performed similarly to controls in the forwards spans; however, performance in both verbal and visuo-spatial backwards conditions were grossly impaired. Although other authors have also reported that differences can be found in forwards spans as a function of increasing chronological age of the children (Hulme & Mackenzie, 1992; Marinosson, 1974), these data clearly indicate that more controlled WM functions may be responsible for the cognitive impairments in DS subjects. We therefore have elements to examine the combination of a differentiation concerning modality specific processes (verbal vs. visuo-spatial), and a differentiation between various levels of control. We have recently studied these aspects in a series of researches with groups of mentally retarded, mainly DS, individuals. We have found that mental retardation is generally associated with WM difficulties. Regardless of the characteristics of the material being used, WM difficulties increase as a function of the level of control/activity required by the task (Tressoldi & Cornoldi, 2000).

Vicari and colleagues (2000b) replicated these findings, indicating a substantial equivalence between verbal and visuo-spatial performance in DS subjects. To investigate this issue further, procedures evaluating explicit and implicit memory functions have been adopted. Explicit tests such as the Corsi Supraspan test, word or picture recognition tasks, and word-list learning have been proposed, together with a battery of implicit tasks such as stem completion, the Fragmented Pictures test, a modified version of the Tower of London test, and the Serial Reaction Time test. Results indicate that DS and control groups perform similarly in implicit memory tests while significant differences emerge in the explicit memory conditions. Once again, no differences emerge between verbal and visuo-spatial tasks. The dissociation between implicit and explicit memory performance is not confined to DS individuals: both developmental and neuropsychological evidence has been reported in this direction (Cermak, 1993; Light & La Voie, 1993). Explicit memory tests place a higher load on attentional resources, both in the encoding and retrieval processes (Carlesimo et al., 1996; Parkin & Russo, 1990) and this could affect subjects' performance.

In conclusion, DS individuals do not always seem to suffer from specific visuo-spatial limitation, although their performance is frequently lower than controls in both verbal and visuo-spatial tasks. The consequences of DS are more evident in highly demanding tasks, involving central executive functions in a WM paradigm. Empirical data confirm that mental retardation cannot be considered as a unitary concept; if anything—in contrast with Uecker and colleagues' (1993) hypotheses—DS individuals seem to show a relative preservation of visuo-spatial abilities when compared to other forms of mental retardation resulting from genetic dysfunction, such as Williams syndrome (Jarrold, Baddeley, & Hewes, 1999; Klein & Mervis, 1999; Wang & Bellugi, 1994). Two studies by Lanfranchi, Cornoldi, and Vianello (2002a, 2002b) examined the WM difficulties of mentally retarded children and, in particular, of DS children within a continuity model framework. In a first study (Lanfranchi et al., 2002b), a subgroup of 17 DS children included in a larger group of mentally retarded children presented a lower performance than a group of typically developing children matched for mental age in all the verbal working memory tasks that were proposed, but the gap between the two groups increased in correspondence with increases in the degree of required control. In a second study (Lanfranchi et al., 2002a), 22 DS children, with a mean chronological age of 14 years and a mean mental age of 4 years and 6 months, and controls matched for mental age, were administered a series of five VSWM tests, all based on the presentation of a 4 × 4 matrix but implying an increase in the required control. The most passive task (level of control 1) required recollection of locations presented simultaneously; the task at level 2 required recollection of a pathway presented sequentially; the level-3 task required recollection of a similar pathway but in backwards order; the level-4 task presented either one or two pathways and required selective recall of only the first position(s) of the pathway(s); the level-5 task involved the same task as at level 4 but also required the subject to tap on the table when the pathway involved a red cell in the matrix. Data from this study are presented in Figure 7.1. Although DS children were no poorer than

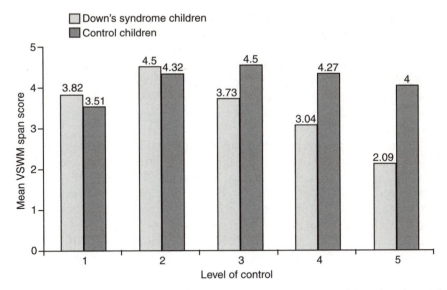

Figure 7.1. Mean visuo-spatial working memory (VSWM) span scores of Down's and control children as a function of the level of required control (1 = very low, 2 = low, 3 = medium, 4 = high, 5 = very high) (from Lanfranchi et al., 2002b).

controls in the most passive tasks, their difficulty increased in the more controlled tasks. The absence of difference in the most passive tasks could be due to the low discriminative power of those tasks. However, Lanfranchi and co-authors found that mentally retarded children with fragile-X syndrome were poorer than controls in these tasks.

The data produced by Lanfranchi and co-authors are important because they show the interaction between modality effects (greater difficulty with verbal material) and control (greater difficulty with higher control), and so confirm the hypothesis that the intellectual deficit present in mental retardation is related to WM control (see also Kane et al., 2001) and that different genetic subgroups within mental retardation can be distinguished according to the modality.

WILLIAMS SYNDROME

Williams syndrome (WS) was originally identified by Williams, Barratt-Boyes, and Lowe in 1961; it has often been identified under the broad term "infantile hypercalcaemia" because of the associated presence of high calcium levels in the blood. The genetic origin of this syndrome was demonstrated only in 1993 (Ewart et al., 1993), when a microdeletion of a portion of chromosome 7 was identified. As well as cardiovascular problems, similarities in physical anomalies are also present: irregular dentition, a depressed nasal bridge, and thick lips result in the typical "elfin profile" (Jones & Smith, 1995). Recent findings also indicate the underlying causes of hyperacusis and hypertension in WS, with high levels of nerve growth factor (Calamandrei et al., 2000). WS produces striking similarities in both physical appearance and associated cognitive profile, with a selective impairment of visuo-spatial abilities; verbal processes are spared. Thus, although WS has only recently been identified, the clear-cut cognitive pattern—quite rare in mental retardation—has been explored in many studies.

Language abilities are usually relatively preserved in WS (Bellugi, Sabo, & Vaid, 1988; Grant et al., 1997), although access to lexical knowledge could be partially impaired (Vicari, Carlesimo, Brizzolara, & Pezzini, 1996a). Some authors also have suggested that the characteristic pattern of flawless verbal performance associated with a marked deficit in visuo-spatial processes could be the result of a faster rate of development of verbal functions compared with nonverbal abilities (Jarrold, Baddeley, & Hewes, 1998). By contrast, Volterra and colleagues (Volterra, Longobardi, Pezzini, Vicari, & Antenore, 1999) recently investigated a case of dizygotic twins, where the male was affected by WS and the female developed at the normal rate. The authors reported that both verbal and nonverbal abilities developed at a slower rate in the WS twin. The two children performed similarly in certain selected tasks only: verbal fluency, memory for phonologically similar words, and face recognition. Both twins had a cognitive profile with good lexical comprehension and, quite surprisingly, the female twin showed a relative weakness in visuo-spatial abilities. In sum, despite isolated contrasting or unclear results (see, for example, Pezzini, Vicari, Volterra, Milani, & Ossella, 1999), there is broad evidence suggesting a selective visuo-spatial deficit associated with WS and it is worth analysing this in more detail.

Bellugi and colleagues (1988) described a heterogeneous pattern in which WS children clearly failed in most visuo-spatial tasks, with selective areas of sparing. WS produced a gross impairment in tasks requiring spatial construction and transformation, as well as in line orientation tasks such as the Benton Line Orientation test. However, facial recognition was spared and also more peripheral perceptual processes did not show any deficit; visuomotor/constructive abilities also seemed to be spared. While drawing from memory was impaired, copying was preserved. Drawing problems have also been reported by Bertrand and collaborators (Bertrand & Mervis, 1996; Bertrand, Mervis, & Eisenberg, 1997), who confirmed WS problems in drawing skills but also indicated a longitudinal improvement in WS individuals, indicating that a normal developmental course of learning is possible. The possibility of distinguishing between an intact visual WM component and an impaired spatial component in WS children was further documented by Vicari, Bellucci, and Carlesimo (in press).

Vicari and colleagues (Vicari, Brizzolara, Carlesimo, Pezzini, & Volterra,

1996b) specifically contrasted short- and long-term retention with verbal and visuo-spatial material in a population of WS individuals. Results confirm a pronounced impairment in visuo-spatial processing in both short- and long-term memory conditions. A dissociation between preserved immediate verbal recall and impaired long-term learning was also reported. These data confirm the general pattern and also confirmed that a greater contribution of lexical–semantic knowledge could result in a decrement in performance with verbal material (Vicari et al., 1996b). A dissociation within visuo-spatial abilities in children with WS is also described by Udwin and Yule (1991), who reported that visual recall and face-recognition skills are preserved whereas spatial relocation, WISC-R performance tasks, and card-sorting tasks are grossly impaired. WS children also show some emotional and behavioural inadequacies, with high levels of anxiety and concentration difficulties (Udwin & Yule, 1991).

We outlined above the hypothesis that DS children could have a selective impairment in processing local features but preserved global analysis. In WS the pattern seems completely reversed: A deficit in spatial construction could be associated with an impairment in global organisation (Bihrle et al., 1989). This issue has been taken further by Pani, Mervis, and Robinson (1999), who used a test requiring a spontaneous global organisation with a sample of WS individuals. Results indicate that WS does not preclude an efficient global organisation of stimuli. However, subjects show a clear weakness in shifting from global to local processing, thus suggesting that the problem does not arise in the presence of a specific level of organisation but from the need to modify the level of processing chosen.

Superficial similarities and marked differences between DS and WS, as well as similarities with some neurological impairments, have led researchers to link WS to right-hemisphere damage conditions and DS to left-hemisphere damage conditions. Although superficial—neither WS nor DS have ever been associated with any kind of neurological damage—functional analogies are present (Jarrold et al., 1999; Klein & Mervis, 1999; Wang & Bellugi, 1994). WS is related to a more distinctive association of perceptual abilities where preserved facial discrimination is associated with generally disrupted perceptual skills (Wang et al., 1995), possibly suggesting a dissociation that maps onto the object/visual vs. spatial pathways in the visual cortex.

FRAGILE-X SYNDROME

Fragile-X syndrome (FXS) is a genetic disorder in which a portion of a gene lengthens significantly, producing failure in RNA transcription. While identification of the fragile site dates back to 1943 (Martin & Bell, 1943), the mutant gene has only recently been identified (Hagerman & Cronister, 1996). Like other genetic dysfunctions, cognitive deficits are present and severe.

Earlier hypotheses of a general and undifferentiated impairment have now been replaced by a number of studies suggesting that a substantial preservation of verbal skills is associated with a weaker performance in visuo-spatial tasks (Crowe & Hay, 1990; Freund & Reiss, 1991), or more generally to deficit in short-term or working memory (Freund & Reiss, 1991; Jakala et al., 1997; Munir, Cornish, & Wilding, 2000).

Studies investigating visuo-spatial impairments in FXS have failed to report general damage to these abilities but rather suggest a relative weakness in visuo-constructive abilities (block design, drawings) together with a performance that does not differ from that of control subjects in tasks requiring facial recognition, visual recognition, visuo-motor control, and visual perception (Cornish, Munir, & Cross, 1998). From a molecular perspective, it is difficult to find an explanation for this selective visuo-constructive impairment. The data are clearly inconsistent with research indicating that the activation ratio (number of normal alleles on X chromosomes) correlates with cognitive performance (Reiss, Freund, Baumgardner, Abrams, & Denckla, 1995) and evidence in the opposite direction (Taylor et al., 1994). Cornish and colleagues (1998) failed to report a correlation between activation ratio and cognitive performance in a large battery of visuo-spatial tasks.

Shapiro and colleagues (Shapiro et al., 1995) reported a dissociation in FXS between preserved verbal digit span and impaired object and block-tapping performance. This study compared the performance of FXS and DS groups, once again indicating that DS coincides with a relative strength in visuo-spatial abilities when compared with other genetic-based manifestations of mental retardation. To further explore verbal and visuo-spatial memory abilities in FXS, Munir and collaborators (2000) carried out an empirical investigation explicitly using a WM theoretical framework. Results show that FXS individuals had an impaired performance in all the different components of WM, phonological loop, VSWM, and central executive. In particular, verbal performance was especially reduced when nonmeaningful material was presented or when complex procedures were adopted (see also Freund & Reiss, 1991). Munir, Cornish, and Wilding (2000) concluded that FXS may produce a general impairment in WM abilities, possibly related to the amount of cognitive resources/executive capacity, irrespective of the WM subsystem. As mentioned in a preceding paragraph, this conclusion was further supported by Lanfranchi and co-authors (2002a) with a battery of VSWM tests requiring different levels of control.

TURNER SYNDROME

Turner syndrome (TS) is another genetic dysfunction associated with the X chromosomes. It is present in females only and is the most common sex-chromosome disorder; one of the X chromosomes is completely or partially deleted (for a review, see Saenger, 1996). First identified by Turner in 1938, the phenotype is characterised by short stature, webbed neck, deformity of the elbows, and gonadal agenesis or dygenesis. From a neurological perspective, different dysfunctions have been reported in different regions of both hemispheres, although the right hemisphere seems to be involved primarily (Rovet, 1995).

A typical cognitive profile of normal IQ and preserved verbal abilities, which may be associated with a reduction in visuo-spatial abilities, is usually associated with TS. The cognitive evaluation of TS has also been made on the basis of a clear-cut discrepancy between verbal and performance IQ (Rovet, 1990). The visuo-spatial weakness is supported by a number of studies showing that TS individuals present selective limitations in tasks requiring spatial memory, visuo-motor integration, or design copying (Buchanan, Pavlovic, & Rovet, 1998). However, contradictory results have also been found and it has been hypothesised that task complexity could be a variable affecting TS performance. Studies on mental rotation may help disentangle this issue. In fact, if stimulus complexity is reduced to a minimum (i.e., simple letter stimuli), differences between TS and control subjects tend to disappear (Murphy et al., 1994), although differences emerge when complex patterns are used (Rovet & Netley, 1982). These data are quite consistent with a selective WM or VSWM impairment in TS (Rovet, 1995), with a specific effect due to the amount of active processing resources required by each task.

In a case study, we carried out an empirical investigation in which four young women with TS undertook a test battery measuring the various aspects of VSWM (Cornoldi, Marconi, & Vecchi, 2001a). All TS individuals showed a normal, or slightly reduced, performance in verbal abilities, measured by verbal spans, memory for abstract words, or analysis of linguistic information. As expected, performance in visuo-spatial tasks was clearly impaired, although the emerging pattern was not homogeneous. In line with Buchanan and colleagues' (1998) data, we did not find a distinction between visual and spatial components of VSWM and, although we did find partial evidence for a dissociation between sequential and simultaneous processing, the results were not conclusive. A pattern of selective, more pronounced deficit seems to emerge. In general, our data support the hypothesis of a pervasive VSWM deficit in TS; however, we also found that the different cognitive profiles of the four girls did not overlap and that each subject could present a specific and typical pattern of performance. These data are coherent with a theoretical interpretation of cognitive deficits in TS that identify two different underlying causes: An organisational defect could be the result of genetic malformations, while an activational defect could reflect a hormonal insufficiency (Rovet, 1995). More recently, Bishop, Canning, Elgar, Morris, Jacobs, and Skuse (2000) suggested that one or more imprinted genes on the X chromosome could affect a different neurological development associated with memory functions. The combination of different underlying mechanisms could then result in marked individual differences in the cognitive profiles associated with TS, within a general weakness in visuo-spatial abilities.

CONCLUDING REMARKS

The investigation of WM deficit in genetic syndromes has contributed to the empirical evidence showing a functional dissociation of components within memory systems. Different syndromes cannot be considered as unique conditions producing mental retardation, but each produces a specific cognitive pattern. In many cases, it is possible to distinguish between verbal and visuo-spatial functions, as well as between more peripheral modality-specific abilities and more central processes. There are syndromes, such as Down's syndrome, in which the cognitive correlates are rather unclear. In some cases specific visuo-spatial difficulties are found, although deficits are usually more evident in the verbal domain. Recent studies highlight that more central, control processes are usually disrupted and that individuals with Down's syndrome present a general WM deficit. Similar evidence is reported in the case of the fragile-X syndrome. Although a selective deficit of visuo-spatial functions have been reported in the past, more recent data indicate that short-term or WM processes must be considered globally, and are generally impaired.

A more specific profile is present in both Williams or Turner syndromes, where a selective preservation of verbal skills is associated with a reduction in visuo-spatial abilities. This seems to be evident in both WM abilities and long-term memory functions. We undertook a detailed investigation of cognitive profiles in women with TS and we could not suggest a specific pattern of impairment in all individuals. Either passive or active processes could be selectively compromised, providing additional evidence for the importance of distinguishing these two aspects of memory processing and the independence of the control/activity dimension from an analysis of task complexity.

CHAPTER EIGHT

A continuity approach to visuo-spatial working memory

As we have seen in the preceding chapters, a series of problems remain unsolved in the study of WM and VSWM. In particular, the "architecture" of the system is still unclear, with a conflict in theories between a "unique structure" view and an opposing view that divides the system into a large series of independent processing subsystems. This problem becomes particularly relevant for the study of VSWM, the organisation and specific properties of which are still to be better defined.

It is unclear which factor produces individual differences, and the question of whether individual differences in WM can all be attributed to the same underlying factor, or if it is also possible that, in some cases, more than one important factor contributes to interindividual variability, remains to be explored.

CONTINUITIES OF MIND

The debate concerning continuities and discontinuities of mind has concerned all areas of psychology, including psychopathology (Kazdin & Kagan, 1994). In general, according to the discontinuous view, psychological dimensions can be considered to be discrete and categorical, with cases potentially falling unquestionably into one category or another. On the contrary, according to the continuous view, different categories are only a convention and are specified by ill-defined borders, as the underlying psychological dimension is a continuous one and all values along the dimension can be assumed by an exemplar, which is the cut-off plausibly, but arbitrarily, defined.

Although continuous and discontinuous perspectives could both be adequate for different contexts and goals, there is evidence that many psychological dimensions are continuous in nature. When applied to the field of memory, the debate appears more problematic as many popular approaches to memory are apparently based on categorical discontinuous dimensions. Experimental and neuropsychological evidence has stressed the need for strong differentiations between different types of memory (Schacter & Tulving, 1994) such as procedural vs. declarative, implicit vs. explicit, semantic vs. episodic, short-term vs. long-term memory, and so on. These distinctions, sometimes originally proposed as heuristics for exploring different aspects of memory, have finally assumed the configuration of separate ontological entities, whose separation has acquired legitimacy from neuropsychological evidence, apparently showing complete dissociation between separate processes. Despite the strengths and popularity associated with a discontinuous view, the opposite continuous view is attracting more and more attention. Throughout this volume we have offered suggestions in favour of a continuous view. In particular, we have mentioned positions arguing against too radical a separation between long- and short-term memory (Cowan, 1995).

A CONTINUITY MODEL OF WORKING MEMORY

On the basis of the available evidence, we (Cornoldi, 1995; Cornoldi & Vecchi, 2000) have developed a modified model of WM assuming that it is necessary to postulate the articulation of the WM system according to continua, distinguishing between parts of the system devoted to different types of processing and to different information modalities.

The aim of our model was to overcome the difficulties of models based either on the assumption of a single comprehensive system (Pascual-Leone, 1987), which does not explain the material-specific effects reported in WM literature, or on the fractionation of a number of independent components (Baddeley, 1986), which does not explain the relationship between components.

Difficulties with a single unitary view of WM emerge on the basis of an impressive amount of experimental evidence. For example, studies using a selective interference paradigm (Brooks, 1968) have repeatedly shown that a secondary concurrent WM task can produce different degrees of interference on a primary WM task, according not only to the similarity of the material but also to the sharing of specific WM resources (see Baddeley, 1986, for a review). The study of individual differences has been critical for the differentiation of cognitive abilities, including components of WM. For example, psychometric evidence shows that different WM tests can be modestly correlated and that the correlations are particularly low when different aspects of WM are measured (Shah & Miyake, 1996). Also, neuropsychological dissociations between different types of WM dysfunction offer evidence in favour of an articulation of the WM system (see Denes & Pizzamiglio, 1999, for a review). As we have shown in the preceding chapters, the study of specific subgroups of individuals shows that WM failures may concern visuo-spatial components but not other aspects of WM. The case of developmental populations with cognitive disabilities is illuminating in this respect (Cornoldi, Carretti, & De Beni, 2001b; Swanson & Siegel, 2001). In particular, it seems possible to find subgroups with difficulties associated with both a specific modality and a particular degree of control. Some children with specific learning disabilities (e.g., dyslexia) have a low performance in passive verbal spans but not in active verbal spans, whereas the opposite can be found in very pure reading comprehension disabilities. However, neither group may have particular difficulties with spatial spans, nor with tasks assumed to measure central functions of mind (Cornoldi, De Beni, & Pazzaglia, 1996b; De Beni et al., 1998). On the contrary, nonverbal learning-disabled children (see Chapter 4) may meet difficulties in active or passive visuo-spatial WM tasks, but not in the corresponding verbal ones, nor in intelligence tests.

As Baddeley (1986) has argued, the functional characteristics of a WM system, that is, its capacity not only to retain information for a short period, but also to use, transform, and integrate it to produce an output that is different from the original data, determines the necessity to integrate in the WM model both the features of peripheral processes that maintain information in WM and the features of more central processes that allow a controlled manipulation of information. However, we assume that controlled WM processes can maintain some modality-specific features. This assumption is not clearly developed in some WM approaches (for a discussion, see Miyake, 2001) although it is considered in Baddeley's group model, but only with reference to active maintenance processes, and in particular to articulatory rehearsal and to the activity of the inner scribe (Logie, 1995). In our view, these latter processes represent examples of modestly active modality-specific processes at a rather low level of a control/activity continuum. This continuum, at higher control levels, is involved in other modality-specific tasks, such as the Listening Span task (Daneman & Carpenter, 1980) and mental rotation tasks. Unlike Baddeley's group approach, we assume that these tasks reflect controlled operations, and are then disturbed by high-control concurrent operations, but that they cannot be referred to a single central control system because they appear in many respects to have different and specific functional properties.

Our model is presented in Figure 8.1. It is characterised by two fundamental dimensions based on continuum relations: the horizontal continuum, related to the different types of material (e.g., verbal, visual, spatial, haptic),

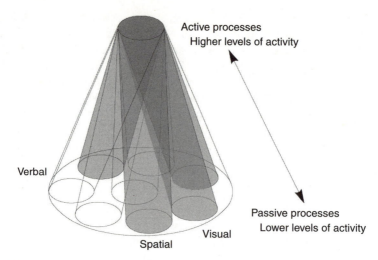

Figure 8.1. Schematic representation of the continuity model of working memory (adapted from Cornoldi, 1995; Cornoldi & Vecchi, 2000; Vecchi, Phillips, & Cornoldi, 2001).

and the vertical continuum, related to the type of process and requiring more or less active elaboration and integration between information from different sources. Each process is then defined on the basis of these two dimensions and the degree of independence between tasks is represented as a distance between positions in the model. The conical structure suggests that greater distances between modalities are postulated in passive, peripheral processes, in contrast with high-level active tasks. At a peripheral level it is also possible to hypothesise completely independent subsystems that are related to early processing of perceptual inputs. Part of the cone has been delineated in black and white to indicate the amount of global cognitive resources required by a certain level or type of process. In fact, as the system is unitary, we assume that the different parts share a single pool of resources. However, as the system is also articulated, we assume that each point of the system has specific local resources. These resources, which can be assumed to be able to reach the same amount at each different location of the WM system, vary in each individual in each location, according to the individual's specific characteristics.

Figure 8.1 also presents examples of different processes, distinguished according to their modality on a horizontal plane, representing a series of horizontal modality-dependent continua. They are also distinguished according to the degree of control along the vertical continuum. Furthermore, a continuity approach to WM also applies to its relationship with other cognitive systems, such as input systems (e.g., language and visuo-spatial information processing) and long-term memory.

In our view, the hypothesis of an unitary articulated approach to WM has a series of important theoretical implications. In particular, it implies that common rules may govern different parts of the system, as we suggested in our consideration of the analogies between properties of the verbal and visuo-spatial portions of the system (see Chapter 2).

In a WM model that postulates independent components, similarities between them can be neither logically deduced nor easily explained. On the contrary, a continuum model is based on the assumption that distant processes could also share functional properties and principles. Along the vertical dimension, similarities are related to the specific characteristics of the information modality. Each process at different points of the horizontal plane is related to other similar processes along the vertical dimension, varying in degree of active processing required. For example, spatial simultaneous processes at different levels of the vertical continuum share common properties related to simultaneous spatiality.

Other analogies and similarities can be found at the horizontal level. For example, at the very low level of the various passive modality-specific components, mainly related to simple storage tasks, effects that could be found in verbal memory tasks (e.g., memory decreases due to unattended speech or phonological similarity; see Baddeley, 1986) have a sibling in visuo-spatial processing that is the effects of visual noise and visual similarity (Logie, 1995). Similarly, at higher control levels the efficiency of inhibitory processes controlling for interference due to irrelevant information appears crucial for both active verbal and visuo-spatial processes. However, similarities do not exclude differences or peculiarities, as is seen in the case of rehearsal processes devoted to refreshing information maintained in WM. Kemps (1999) recently highlighted that mechanisms for verbal and spatial rehearsal differ in part. In fact, verbal rehearsal is related to speech articulation (Baddeley, Thomson, & Buchanan, 1975), whereas a mirroring mechanism for VSWM cannot be found easily. It is possible to suggest that a general rehearsing capacity might combine with different material (e.g., verbal, visual, spatial) to give rise to similar, but peculiar and specific, processes. Research has shown that the rehearsal mechanism in the articulatory loop is disturbed by articulatory suppression and, in VSWM rehearsal, is disturbed by spatial tapping. It could then be assumed that the mechanism responsible for VSWM rehearsal reflects the characteristics of spatial tapping. However, this conclusion is still in need of experimental evidence and it might be unable to explain how people maintain nonspatial patterns in VSWM (e.g., the image of an object or a coloured surface). In fact, it has been suggested that visual noise interferes with visuo-spatial passive tasks and spatial tapping with more active processes (Logie, 1995). However, visual noise seems to be associated with visual rather than passive processes. For example, Quinn and McConnell (1996; McConnell & Quinn, 2000) found that multiple interactive images, a very high-level active process, were disturbed by visual noise, and that spatial tapping disturbed spatial rather than active processes.

GLOBAL AND LOCAL COGNITIVE RESOURCES IN THE CONTINUOUS WM SYSTEM AND SOURCES OF INDIVIDUAL DIFFERENCES

Our framework relies on the concept of cognitive resources. This concept, although popular and intuitively evident, raises a number of theoretical problems (see, for example, Salthouse, 1991). Cognitive resources define the system capacity: A task can be performed if the system has sufficient resources. This assumption is consistent with the idea of resources that implies they are not infinite, and with the general assumption in cognitive science that systems have a limited capacity.

In our view (Cornoldi & Vecchi, 2000), it is possible to distinguish between specific resources conceded to each position of the system (values $n1$, $n2$, etc., associated with the resources that are necessary to carry out specific tasks) and the global quantity of resources available to the overall WM system. Each task $X1$ is related to a specific amount of cognitive resources $n1$, which is associated with the corresponding position in the system. This does not mean that another task $X2$ could simply require $n2$ independent resources. As a logical consequence of a continuum model, the resources still available for $X2$ will be related to the distance between $X1$ and $X2$. In fact, $n2$ is dependent on $n1$ and a greater distance between the tasks will result in a greater number of available resources. Therefore, the possibility for two tasks to be carried out together is related to the distance between the tasks and, as a consequence, the available resources.

The global quantity of resources that can be used for each couple of tasks can then be defined as $N = n1 + n2d + nt$, where d = dependent on the distance from $n1$ and nt defines the additional resources required to carry out more than one task at the same time. However, we should hypothesise not only a limited quantity of resources for each position of the system but also a general capacity of WM system defined by an amount, T, of resources.

Logically, the amount T must not be inferior to the amount N. Two cognitive tasks could be performed together with more or less difficulty, depending on their position on the vertical continuum: Two passive tasks require a low amount of resources and, even with the additional nt, the global amount is likely to be less than T. This would not be true in the case of active tasks.

This framework helps an understanding of why two distant tasks with a similar position on one continuum but varying in their passive/active nature may show wide-ranging effects of selective interference. The presence of interference effects is related to: (1) the quantity, N, of requested resources; (2) distance on the vertical continuum; and (3) distance on the horizontal continuum. For example, an individual can cope quite easily with two passive WM tasks, one verbal and the other visuo-spatial, because the two corresponding WM components may use different local resources and the resources subtracted are not particularly high, presumably below the total amount, T, of resources available to the system. However, the individual may meet severe difficulties in coping simultaneously with two active tasks (e.g., a mental rotation and a random generation task) because their distance is smaller and one task partially subtracts resources from the other (due to a reduction in distances between different modalities at higher levels of the cone), and because the local required resources are high and may go beyond the total amount, T, of available resources.

This resource view can be used to examine the issue of individual differences. In fact, these differences could be due to either a low degree of available local resources at one or more points in the WM system (as happens in people with specific failures) or to a lower degree of available overall resources. This latter circumstance can be found in people with more general cognitive impairments, like mentally retarded individuals who show impairments in nearly all WM tasks, but also meet increasing difficulty in correspondence with the increase in degree of control (and then of resources request) implied by the task (Lanfranchi, Cornoldi, & Vianello, 2002). On the contrary, individuals within normal populations, or other groups of subjects, seem to present limitations in specific points of the WM system. In this book we have reviewed the case of single groups of individuals who present, often but not necessarily always, typical patterns of difficulty in WM tasks. These difficulties mainly concern active components of VSWM. The prevalence of active VSWM deficits in the groups we have reviewed may be due to the fact that, according to our model, active components are generally more vulnerable than passive ones. In fact, active components are involved in more demanding tasks than passive components. There is then a higher probability of having an insufficient amount of n resources to carry out the tasks.

The repeated findings of difficulties in VSWM tasks not associated with difficulty in the corresponding verbal active tasks is important because it confirms that these tasks cannot be referred to the same control mechanism. It must also be noted that an apparently similar pattern of difficulty concerning active VSWM in different groups of individuals may conceal important differences. The difficulties of the congenitally totally blind are obviously due to a lack of experience, which may also compromise the development of specialised cognitive structures. These factors are evidently different from those affecting the difficulties shown by female individuals (see Vecchi, 2001). Different again are the VSWM difficulties of the elderly, presumably associated with variations in local n resources as well as the T global resources.

This resource view does not contradict other views of individual differences in WM (Miyake, 2001; see also Chapter 2) as it assumes that storage and processing resources are part of a unique system, and coping simultaneously with different tasks produces a further subtraction of resources. We agree that control (including inhibition of irrelevant information) is critical to success in WM tasks, especially the active ones. In particular, our view is shared by the "controlled attention" perspective proposed by Engle's group (Engle, Tuholski, Laughlin, & Conway, 1999b), such as the unitary view—the idea that it is possible to distinguish between modality-specific storage functions and less modal control, the reference of inhibitory mechanisms to the general control functions. However, from our position, control is associated to, but not identified with, attention (complex passive tasks may require more attention than simple active tasks) and the WM control varies along a continuum maintaining modality-specific features, although in a reduced way.

As we have discussed in Chapters 2, 5 and 6, we think that the effects of high automatisation as a consequence of very prolonged experience with a task can be considered orthogonal to each point of the WM system, implying a reduced demand on resources. We think that the role of experience and strategies are intriguing variables for each approach analysing individual differences in WM. In fact, these aspects can be only partially considered as simply orthogonal to WM components. For example, experience can also affect the availability of local resources, as we have seen in the case of the blind and local active visuo-spatial resources. The use of adequate strategies can also depend on both experience and the quantity of available resources, as people with a greater number of resources can probably afford a higher use of controlled strategies.

Within this view, there is still a need to identify the specific mechanisms and factors, which—as a result of a lack of resources—produce individual failures in WM tasks. Poor inhibitory mechanisms, difficulties in transforming information, and scarce use of strategies, for example, may contribute to WM failures. Individual differences in WM probably cannot all be attributed to the same underlying factor and it is also possible that, in some cases, more than one important factor contributes to interindividual variability.

VERTICAL CONTINUUM: PROCESSING-DEPENDENT FEATURES

Positions on the vertical continuum represent the amount of activity/control requested by the corresponding cognitive operations and associated tasks. The position of a cognitive operation along the continuum is related to the degree of active control it requires.

In the tripartite model of WM (Baddeley, 1986), the vertical continuum could be represented by the degree of coordination between central components (central executive) and more peripheral subsystems (articulatory loop and visuo-spatial sketch pad). However, the conceptualisation of continua is more economical, more flexible, and allows us to identify a different amount of central control in each task. In our view it is not possible to hypothesise tasks performed, for example, through the peripheral subsystems only, and tasks requiring the involvement of both central and peripheral structures. WM is a unitary system and it is implied as a whole. The characteristics of the continuum do not allow an interruption between central and peripheral structures and it is then possible to determine a role for control processes in a large number of tasks. This hypothesis is coherent with experimental findings indicating that tasks traditionally associated with the central executive, like random generation, nevertheless involve an important role for the peripheral subsystems. We can consider tasks such as verbal comprehension and mental rotation as examples of tasks producing difficulties for a tripartite model. In both cases, it is impossible to assign these tasks to peripheral subsystems only, although a specific role of information-specific structures, verbal and visuo-spatial, is clearly evident. Thus, WM theorists had to modify the original assumption regarding an independent role for peripheral structures in such tasks, and postulated an involvement of the central executive as soon as the task became too complex to be assigned to a peripheral subsystem only. Although it is impossible to identify the level of complexity that requires the activation of the central executive, several studies have confirmed that even the central process can maintain some level of material-dependent specificity, as shown in the results reported by Daneman and colleagues. In 1980, Daneman and Carpenter devised a procedure—the Listening Span task—that, unlike other simpler forms of verbal span, required a higher level of processing and was connected to central executive functions. Several years later, Daneman and Tardif (1987) compared these tasks with other measures of central processing involving visuo-spatial material and did not report a substantial correlation.

Data obtained by Miyake and co-authors could be interpreted within this framework. Shah and Miyake (1996) confirmed some independence between central verbal and visuo-spatial tasks. Furthermore, Miyake et al. (2001) found that three different spatial tasks (Spatial Visualisation, Spatial Relations, and Perceptual Speed) shared some commonalities, but were also distinguishable, as they loaded on three correlated but distinguishable factors. Furthermore, structural equation modelling suggested that the three factors differed in the degree of executive control involvement, lowest for Perceptual Speed and highest for Spatial Visualisation.

In our own studies, we (Cornoldi et al., 1991a) have demonstrated that an impairment in central tasks based on visuo-spatial material does not imply similar limitations in central verbal tasks. This point is clearly consistent with the existence of both global and local resources.

A model of WM based upon continua, and specifically the characteristics of the vertical continuum, does not lead to different predictions from a more traditional view of WM based on independent components. Logie, for example (Logie, 1995; Duff & Logie, 2001), suggests that every task may require an integration of peripheral and central processing, thus suggesting that the central executive is a mere mechanism for allocating cognitive resources to the different subsystems. The central executive has been considered responsible for various tasks (e.g., random generation) and therefore a unique system should be considered both as a control/attentional mechanism and as a real component performing a task.

We believe that a continuity model could explain the functioning of the system better. First, the conceptualisation of different continua helps us interpret the results obtained in different tasks, implicitly showing the different degree of required control. Second, in our perspective we are not obliged to limit the interrelations of functions required by each task. Verbal, visuo-spatial, and central aspects could be involved together, for example in a reading comprehension task, with combinations of horizontal (modality-dependent) and vertical (process-dependent) features. Third, a continuum organisation does not necessarily suggest a specific structure for the central component, thus excluding theoretical faults in considering it both as an attentional mechanism and as a component responsible for specific tasks. Finally, the vertical continuum hypothesises two extreme levels—often identified as the passive and the active poles. At the same time, it considers each task (and the corresponding WM operations) as an intermediate case between the passive and active poles and, consequently, as a specific position on the continuum.

The relationship between passive and active (which are in fact mainly passive or mainly active tasks) could well describe the characteristics of the vertical continuum. It is clearly impossible to define a task as being completely passive or completely active. Every task has a degree of active control, even if minimal (as in the case of very passive storage tasks). Therefore, each task can be associated with a specific position along the vertical continuum, and this position identifies the specific level of activity/control. Some tasks could be more active, whereas others require simpler, more passive processes. The amount of integration, modification, or transformation of stimuli may be associated with the position on the vertical continuum.

Consider a passive task such as the digit span, for example. This is definitely a passive task in our definition (memorisation and recall of stimuli in the same format) but we cannot assume that it is positioned at the maximum passive level. The task may require mental rehearsal of the stimuli and thus a peculiar combination of passive and active processes. However, we would suggest a position on the continuum quite close to the passive pole, as active/mental rehearsal is a form of active processing that is very far from the active pole. Higher levels are requested when tasks require the manipulation and transformation of information such as in mental rotation or mental synthesis tasks.

The existence of a vertical continuum is associated with the possibility of identifying the variables affecting the position between the passive and the active poles. The passive/active distinctions could well apply to explaining the general function of the system but we still need to define the characteristics that make a task more or less active.

It could be suggested that the level of controlled activity is the variable affecting the continuum. The level attained by a specific operation can be individuated by an analysis and taxonomy of WM operations. For example, we acknowledge that simple mental rehearsal does not necessarily require higher level of activation. Conversely, we can consider the situation in which a subject is required to mentally transform the list of material originally presented. In 1998, Belleville and colleagues (Belleville, Rouleau, & Caza, 1998) proposed a modified verbal span in which participants had to remember a list of words but recall them in alphabetical order. In the traditional verbal span there is a low-level mental rehearsal, whereas in the alphabetical span a much higher level of activation is required. Similarly, we could analyse a visual recognition task that requires two identical configurations to be matched, and an active sibling in which the second stimulus is presented upside-down, rotated through 180°. The first task is simple, mainly passive; the second requires rather complex manipulation and a much higher level of activity. An example of a study based on task taxonomy is by Lanfranchi and colleagues (2002a), who assumed that mentally retarded people would show increasing difficulty, independently of modality, but corresponding to increased degree of required control, moving from very low control (forwards word span), to slightly higher control (backwards word span), to a greater control (listening span), to an even higher control (span with a dual-task request).

An associated variable affecting the continuum is the degree of elaborative integration required by each task. Stimuli can be integrated following different sensory inputs (integration of auditory and visual stimuli, for example) or from long-term memory stores. The generation of mental images is an example of a task generally requiring a high degree of elaborative integration. Visual, verbal, and other sources should be integrated to generate the corresponding image and the request for cognitive resources is obviously high. As a consequence, the nature of the material involved and the characteristics of the task to be performed determine the overall process and the degree of integration required. At the same time, stimuli from long-term stores can influence the type of process and determine the level on the vertical continuum. Long-term information can be used for simple object or face recognition tasks and also for complex integration of stimuli.

The position on the vertical continuum varies in relation to the degree of activity/control required by each task and this is correlated with the number of cognitive resources required at that level. Each task is then a function both of level of resources and position on the continuum. Another example of a cognitive task placing a high load on the WM system is mental rotation (in fact, this aspect is reflected by the importance that this and other tasks assume in the interpretation of individual differences in visuo-spatial abilities). Mental rotation requires the manipulation of different information, varying on the basis of the type of material (2D or 3D, for example), familiarity with the task, and specific strategies that each individual may adopt. In addition, subjects are requested to inhibit the initial configuration and generate the new one in rotated axes, and the ability to select and inhibit information is widely considered as an example of central WM processes (Hasher & Zacks, 1988). Overall, the task requires a large number of resources and it can be positioned at a high level on the continuum, with potentially important variations according to specific manipulations (Just, Carpenter, Maguire, Diwadkar, & McMains, 2001). Mental rotation can then be considered as a mainly active task, typically visuo-spatial, and different from other mainly active tasks that involve verbal material, such as the Listening Span task (Daneman & Carpenter, 1980). The level on the continuum could be similar but the allocation of resources varies. Global resources are the same, whereas the required local resources are more dependent on the characteristics of the material. The allocation of resources, and consequently the possibility of dissociating different functions, is a matter in which the characteristics of the active continuum are dependent on the horizontal continuum and vice versa. Similar vertical levels may be related to different horizontal positions and then imply different local resources but similar global requests.

Finally, it must be noted that the vertical continuum is related to, but cannot be identified with, dimensions like automaticity, complexity, difficulty, request of attention, and storage-processing trade-off. In particular, WM operations are affected by experience and automatisation, but this may happen for each point of the system. For example, either a passive task (like memory for a visual pattern) or a complex task (such as a mental rotation) may be facilitated by experience or even automatisation, but they maintain their position within the WM system, although with a consequent request of energies. In some way, experience and automatisation affect each point of the system orthogonally. Increased task complexity and/or difficulty may involve each point of the continuum similarly. As has been shown by high-complexity requests for WM tasks, the pattern sometimes remains the same even if task difficulty increases (Vecchi et al., 1995). We have seen in the preceding chapters that blind people or elderly individuals may have greater problems with active VSWM tasks than with the passive ones, even if the passive were more difficult and presumably required a high degree of attentional effort.

Finally, although active tasks are characterised by a critical processing component and the passive tasks are typically associated with storage functions, the vertical continuum does not describe the proportional request of storage and processing. In fact, operations with prevalent processing aspects (e.g., repetitive rehearsal) may also be very low in the vertical continuum.

HORIZONTAL CONTINUUM: MODALITY-DEPENDENT FEATURES

The horizontal continuum depends on the specific material used in the task. The dissociation between visual, spatial, or verbal processes are examples of different points along the horizontal continuum. Differences between modality-dependent processes are not only present at peripheral low-level processing but are found at each level of the vertical continuum. Distances between operations of different modalities vary according to vertical positions and this is well represented by the conic structure of the model.

Each task could imply either the use of single-modality information—like the rehearsal of verbal stimuli in a span task—or the integration of different stimuli. For example, the generation of mental images often requires visual, spatial, auditory, and long-term information. The generation of mental images from visual stimuli is not exactly the same process as generation from auditory input. The integration of visual and verbal stimuli implies a greater load on the system, a higher position on the vertical continuum, and a less extreme location on the horizontal continuum.

The existence of material-dependent dissociations is well documented in neuropsychological and experimental studies. At a peripheral level, a portion of the system could be activated automatically from different information. We suggest that the lowest vertical level corresponds to positions in which a complete dissociation between independent systems is possible. These separate components can be interpreted as independent subsystems, or simply as separate peripheral processors.

The horizontal continuum interrupts at the most peripheral level, closely connected with the subsystems receiving direct information from sensory inputs. It is not possible to consider these independent parts of the system as simple sensorial stores, capable of maintaining information for some milliseconds only. It is very likely that, as happens for the other parts of the WM system, they must be connected to information, stored in LTM, which can be used to carry out automatic processes such as object or face recognition. We hypothesise a close bidirectional relationship between WM and LTM: Information stored in LTM can be used for WM processes and the outcome of a WM process can be transferred in LTM. To specify the relationship between WM and LTM, it is possible to hypothesise that the information available from LTM is not similar at all levels of the vertical continuum. In particular, information available at the peripheral levels is fairly limited, whereas a greater load from semantic memory is present in higher processes.

The modality-specific characteristics of the system are present in the horizontal continuum. We hypothesise that, although potentially dissociable, different areas tend to work together in the normal brain and it is then important to understand the nature of relationships. Indirect confirmation on this point comes from analyses of various neuropsychological pathologies, such as prosopagnosia. In this case, people are able to recognise the voice of a well-known person but are not capable of identifying a person visually. The rather peripheral (and often automatised) process of face recognition is compromised and isolated on the vertical continuum. Information from what we see and listen to cannot be matched and integrated in the more complex process of recognising the whole aspects of the person in front of us. To summarise, it is possible to hypothesise that the position on the vertical continuum (level of activity/control) influences the nature of the relationship between WM and LTM. Different information is available from LTM and, conversely, the possibility to store WM outputs in LTM is variable.

Recent theoretical reformulations of WM models suggest that a preliminary semantic, LTM, analysis is critical in the possibility of undertaking a WM process. In our view it is not coherent to hypothesise an undifferentiated role of LTM in every WM process. Logie and Della Sala recently reinterpreted a number of neuropsychological dissociations in patients with unilateral neglect to demonstrate that information that did not reach WM processes is nevertheless encoded in LTM (Beschin, Cocchini, Della Sala, & Logie, 1997). However, this does not necessarily imply that all information receives the same treatment, and it does not give additional information on the sort of LTM processes that are implied. For example, in phonological reading/ surface dyslexia, Marshall and Newcombe (1973) demonstrated that flawless peripheral processes can be associated with an impairment in the semantic access.

A number of classical dissociations have been postulated within the horizontal continuum. One of them is the dissociation between verbal and visuo-spatial material. Verbal and visuo-spatial processes typically represent two distant positions along the continuum. However, we have neuropsychological and experimental evidence (see Chapter 2) of dissociation between much closer points, such as between visual and spatial processes. Visual and spatial processes are largely interconnected in everyday life and this suggests a shorter distance on the horizontal continuum (Pazzaglia & Cornoldi, 1999). Visual stimuli are always located in space and then processed together with their spatial characteristics. These two subsystems usually work together and present a large degree of overlap, although it is still possible to differentiate separate components (Hecker & Mapperson, 1997; Logie & Marchetti, 1991; Luzzatti et al., 1998).

Several dissociations have been proposed within the WM system. Colour, shape, and texture can be processed independently (Davidoff, 1991, 1997) and apparently visual processes can be considered closer to the auditory/ articulatory component, such as the visual recognition of objects. In this case, the verbal description of the object plays an important role in its recognition, and visual and verbal information is likely to be associated in LTM. We have already discussed the distinction proposed by Kosslyn (1994) between categorical and coordinate spatial processes. These abilities can perhaps be differentiated but are certainly interconnected within the visuo-spatial processing system and are thus very close in the horizontal continuum.

In principle, the number of possible dissociations is infinite. However, the possibility of identifying each couple of tasks in terms of a distance along the vertical and the horizontal continua helps in reconsidering the significance of a dissociation within a general cognitive system. Two visuo-spatial processes could be as distant as one visual and one haptic, for example. Each task requires a detailed analysis for its specific characteristics to be understood and for it to be positioned along the vertical and horizontal dimensions. The graphic representation of the model is three-dimensional to account for these aspects.

The structure of the horizontal continuum may also help us to understand the nature of the several dissociations reported within spatial processes— categorical vs. coordinate (Kosslyn, 1994), sequential vs. simultaneous (Pazzaglia & Cornoldi, 1999)—or within some aspects of verbal elaboration—natural sounds vs. auditory linguistic (Tinti et al., 1997).

The conical structure of our model is also intended to show that the distance between processes based upon different inputs (e.g., verbal vs. visual) tends to decrease as soon as the position on the vertical dimension increases. We acknowledge that it is possible to hypothesise the existence of completely independent processes at the most peripheral level. As soon as the amount of active processing increases, the interrelation between the different areas becomes more and more evident. The possibility to distinguish between verbal and visuo-spatial processes, for example, is always present, although two active tasks, one verbal and one spatial, tend to interfere with each other to a greater extent and the degree of independence is rather low.

This assumption is coherent with empirical data and earlier formulations of the WM model. Modality-specific effects in active tasks are fairly limited and active processes per se may be associated with characteristics usually ascribed to the central executive. Two passive tasks are more compatible than two active ones if they are presented in a dual-task condition. This effect can also be interpreted as a function of a shorter or longer distance between the two tasks, or to the extent to which the two tasks share the same underlying cognitive structures. The difficulty of carrying out more than one task at the same time is then dependent on the amount of available cognitive resources.

DISSOCIATING FUNCTIONS, INTEGRATING MODELS

In principle, the continuity model is coherent with an infinite number of distinctions/dissociations within WM. In fact, the more the task is sensitive the more it is possible to differentiate processes, even if they are very close and interconnected. The advantage of our view is that this does not imply an increase in the number of subcomponents and allows us to maintain the economic principle of a unique system in which more or less distant positions are activated from time to time. Within this view, the implications of a dissociation are different from a modular view (Fodor, 1983; Shallice, 1988). A so-called dissociated ability is assumed not to be completely independent of other cognitive abilities, but with an increasing level of relationship to abilities closer to it.

Cognitive neuropsychology is generally more concerned with finding dissociations than similarities. Consequently, neuropsychological models are not typically organised on a continuum basis. This perspective is also due to the specific techniques used, which are able to show differences between processes but do not provide information about the "distance" between them. However, dissociations between processes that are distant in our framework (e.g., verbal and visuo-spatial) are more common than processes that are interrelated (e.g., visual and spatial). This effect is coherent with our view. It can be hypothesised that a brain lesion usually damages not just a single small area of the system but also involves different adjacent areas, both anatomically and functionally. However, even in the case of very specific brain damage reducing WM resources available for operations related to a particular point in the WM system, it can be hypothesised that some difficulties may also be identified for operations associated with close points in the WM system.

Moreover, a dissociation in terms of neurological structures does not necessarily imply that the processes are normally independent in their functioning. Structures that normally work together could be selectively damaged, and this becomes evident in neuropsychological assessment, although it is very difficult to replicate in experimental studies. For example, neuropsychological evidence shows a dissociation between visual and spatial processes (Farah et al., 1988; Luzzatti et al., 1998) but experimental evidence is very limited (Logie & Marchetti, 1991), with some data that are apparently incoherent (Cornoldi et al., 1993; Vecchio, 1991). Various tasks are often carried out by using different combinations of information, for example, a visual and a spatial component cannot be easily distinguished, as a visual object is necessarily perceived and represented in a particular location and is defined by the spatial relationships between its parts; vice versa, a location is identified by a visual point that differentiates it from other locations.

Connectionist approaches to neuropsychology (Haugeland, 1997) appear more compatible with our hypotheses. In fact, in a connectionist model, each WM process can be represented in terms of a specific pattern of activation, overlapping to different extents with other patterns of activation related to other WM tasks.

In conclusion, the architecture of the WM system appears more complex than initially suggested. The complexity of the system is not only a matter of the number of distinct boxes, or relatively independent components. The interrelation between different areas could play the greatest role in our under-standing of WM functioning. We acknowledge that, in principle, empirical evidence cannot successfully resolve the theoretical debate about the existence of continuum vs. discrete dimensions in the system. However, we believe that there are now considerable data showing that a greater articulation of the model is necessary to account for data not only reporting dissociations, but also indicating equivalences, similarities, and specific and general resources. The challenge of future research is to identify all the variables that could affect a processing measure of WM functions and the specific relationships among them.

References

Aleman, A., Van Lee, L., Mantione, M. H. M., Verkoijen, I. G., & De Haan, E. H. F. (2001). Visual imagery without visual experience: Evidence from congenitally blind people. *Neuroreport, 12,* 2601–2604.

Allen, L., Kirasic, K. C., Dobson, S. H., Long, R. G., & Beck, S. (1996). Predicting environmental learning from spatial abilities: An indirect route. *Intelligence, 22,* 327–355.

Allen, P. A., Hall, R. J., Druley, J. A., Smith, A. F., Sanders, R. E., & Murphy, M. D. (2001). How shared are age-related influences on cognitive and noncognitive variables? *Psychology and Aging, 16,* 532–549.

Anastasi, A. (1981) Sex differences: Historical perspectives and methodological implications. *Developmental Review, 1,* 187–206.

Anderson, J. R., Anthouard, M., De-Monte, M., & Kempf, J. (1993). Differences in performance of young and old monkeys on a visuospatial memory task. *Quarterly Journal of Experimental Psychology, 46B,* 391–398.

Ando, J., Ono, Y., & Wright, M. J. (2001). Genetic structure of spatial and verbal working memory. *Behavior Genetics, 31,* 615–624.

Andrade, J. (Ed.) (2001). *Working memory in perspective.* Philadelphia, PA: Psychology Press.

Arditi, A., Holtzman, J. D., & Kosslyn, S. M. (1988). Mental imagery and sensory experience in congenital blindness. *Neuropsychologia, 26,* 1–12.

Arenberg, D. (1978). Differences and changes with age in the Benton Visual Retention Test. *Journal of Gerontology, 33,* 534–540.

Astur, R. S., Ortiz, M. L., & Sutherland, R. J. (1998). A characterization of performance by men and women in a virtual Morris water task: A large and reliable sex difference. *Behavioural Brain Research, 93,* 185–190.

Atkinson, R. C., & Shiffrin, R. M. (1968). Human memory. A proposed system and its control processes. In K. W. Spence & J. T. Spence (Eds.), *The psychology of learning and motivation, 2* (pp. 89–105). New York: Academic Press.

Attneave, F., & Curlee, T. E. (1983). Locational representation in imagery: A moving spot task. *Journal of Experimental Psychology: Human Perception and Performance, 9,* 20–30.

Avons, S. E., & Mason, A. (1999). Effects of visual similarity on serial report and item recognition. *Quarterly Journal of Experimental Psychology*, *52A*, 217–240.

Baddeley, A. D. (1986). *Working memory*. Oxford: Oxford University Press.

Baddeley, A. D. (1990). *Human memory: Theory and practice*. Hove, UK: Lawrence Erlbaum Associates Ltd.

Baddeley, A. D. (1994). Working memory: The interface between memory and cognition. In D. L. Schacter & E. Tulving (Eds.), *Memory systems 1994* (pp. 351–367). Cambridge, MA: MIT Press.

Baddeley, A. D., & Andrade, J. (2000). Working memory and the vividness of imagery. *Journal of Experimental Psychology: General*, *129*, 126–145.

Baddeley, A. D., Bressi, S., Della Sala, S., Logie, R. H., & Spinnler, H. (1991). The decline of working memory in Alzheimer's disease. *Brain*, *114*, 2521–2542.

Baddeley, A. D., & Hitch, G. (1974). Working memory. In G. H. Bower (Ed.), *The psychology of learning and motivation: Advances in research and theory* (Vol. 8, pp. 47–89). New York: Academic Press.

Baddeley, A. D., Logie, R. H., Bressi, S., Della Sala, S., & Spinnler, H. (1986). Dementia and working memory. *Quarterly Journal of Experimental Psychology*, *38A*, 603–618.

Baddeley, A. D., Thomson, N., & Buchanan, M. (1975). Word length and the structure of short-term memory. *Journal of Verbal Learning and Verbal Behavior*, *14*, 575–589.

Baenninger, M., & Newcombe, N. (1989). The role of experience in spatial test performance: A meta-analysis. *Sex Roles*, *20*, 327–344.

Ball, M. J., & Nuttal, K. (1981). Topography of neurofibrillary tangles and granovacuoles in the hippocampi of patients with Down's syndrome: Quantitative comparison with normal ageing and Alzheimer's disease. *Neuropathology and Applied Neurobiology*, *7*, 13–20.

Baltes, P. B., & Baltes, M. M. (Eds.) (1990). *Successful aging*. Cambridge: Cambridge University Press.

Beaumont, J. G. (1988). *Understanding neuropsychology*. Cambridge, MA: Basil Blackwell.

Behrmann, M., Moscovitch, M., & Winocur, G. (1994). Intact visual imagery and impaired visual perception in a patient with visual agnosia. *Journal of Experimental Psychology: Human Perception and Performance*, *20*, 1068–1087.

Belleville, S., Rouleau, N., & Caza, N. (1998). Effect of normal aging on the manipulation of information in working memory. *Memory and Cognition*, *26*, 572–583.

Bellugi, U., Bihrle, A., Jernigan, T., Trauner, D., & Doherty, S. (1990). Neuropsychological, neurological, and neuroanatomical profile of Williams syndrome. *American Journal of Medical Genetics, Suppl. 6*, 115–125.

Bellugi, U., Sabo, H., & Vaid, J. (1988). Spatial deficits in children with Williams syndrome. In J. Stiles-Davis, M. Kritchevsky, & U. Bellugi (Eds.), S*patial cognition: Brain bases and development* (pp. 273–298). Hillsdale, NJ: Lawrence Erlbaum Associates Inc.

Bender, L. (1938). A visual motor Gestalt test and its clinical use. *Research Monographs*, American Orthopsychiatric Association, No. 3, xi + 176.

Bennet, G. K., Seashore, H. G., & Wesman, A. G. (1954). *Differential aptitude tests*. New York: Psychological Corporation.

Benton, A. L. (1959). *Right–left discrimination and finger localisation*. New York: Hoeber-Harper.

Benton, A. L. (1960). *Test de rétention visuelle. Manuel d'application*. Paris: CPA.

Benton, A. L., Hamsher, K. D., Varney, N. R., & Spreen, O. (1983). *Contributions to neuropsychological assessment. A clinical manual*. Oxford: Oxford University Press.

Berch, D. B., Krikorian, R., & Huha, E. M. (1998). The Corsi block-tapping task: Methodological and theoretical considerations. *Brain and Cognition*, *38*, 317–338.

Berenbaum, S. A., & Hines, M. (1992). Early androgens are related to sex-typed toy preferences. *Psychological Science*, *3*, 203–206.

Bertrand, J., & Mervis, C. B. (1996). Longitudinal analysis of drawings by children with Williams syndrome: Preliminary results. *Visual Arts Research*, *22*, 19–34.

Bertrand, J., Mervis, C. B., & Eisenberg, J. D. (1997). Drawing by children with Williams syndrome: A developmental perspective. *Developmental Neuropsychology*, *13*, 41–67.

Beschin, N., Cocchini, G., Della Sala, S., & Logie, R. H. (1997). What the eyes perceive, the brain ignores: A case of pure unilateral representational neglect. *Cortex*, *33*, 3–26.

Bihrle, A., Bellugi, U., Delis, D., & Marks, S. (1989). Seeing either the forest or the trees: Dissociation in visuospatial processing. *Brain and Cognition*, *11*, 37–49.

Bishop, D. V. M., Canning, E., Elgar, K., Morris, E., Jacobs, P. A., & Skuse, D. H. (2000). Distinctive patterns of memory function in subgroups of females with Turner syndrome: Evidence for imprinted loci on the X-chromosome affecting neurodevelopment. *Neuropsychologia*, *38*, 712–721.

Bleecker, M. L., Bolla-Wilson, K., & Meyers, D. A. (1988). Age-related sex differences in verbal memory. *Journal of Clinical Psychology*, *44*, 403–411.

Bosco, A., Cavallini, E., Longoni, A. M., Richardson, J. T. E., & Vecchi, T. (2002). The assessment of active memory processes in old age: A comparison of two tasks. *Brain and Cognition*, *48*, 246.

Braine, L. G. (1978). Early stages in the perception of orientation. In M. Bornter (Ed.), *Cognitive growth and development: Essays in memory of Herbert G. Birch* (pp. 105–133). New York: Brunner/Mazel.

Brainerd, C. J. & Reyna, V. F. (1993). Domains of fuzzy trace theory. In M. L. Hove & R. Pasnak (Eds.), *Emerging themes in cognitive development* (pp. 50–93). New York: Springer-Verlag.

Brandimonte, M., Hitch, G. J., & Bishop, D. (1992a). Influence of short-term memory codes on visual image processing. Evidence from image transformation tasks. *Journal of Experimental Psychology: Learning, Memory, and Cognition*, *18*, 157–165.

Brandimonte, M., Hitch, G. J., & Bishop, D. (1992b). Verbal recoding of visual stimuli impairs mental image transformations. *Memory and Cognition*, *20*, 449–455.

Brooks, L. R. (1968). Spatial and verbal components in the act of recall. *Canadian Journal of Psychology*, *22*, 349–368.

Broverman, D. M., Vogel, W., Klaiber, E. L., Majcher, D., Shea, D., & Paul, V. (1981). Changes to cognitive task performance across the menstrual cycle. *Journal of Comparative and Physiological Psychology*, *95*, 646–654.

Bruner, J. S., Busiek, R. D., & Minturn, A. L. (1952). Assimilation in the immediate reproduction of visually perceived figures. *Journal of Experimental Psychology*, *44*, 151–155.

Bruner, J. S., Olver, R. R., & Greenfield, P. M. (1966). *Studies in cognitive growth: A collaboration at the Center for Cognitive Studies*. New York: John Wiley.

Buchanan, L., Pavlovic, J., & Rovet, J. (1998). A re-examination of the visuospatial deficit in Turner syndrome: Contributions of working memory. *Developmental Neuropsychology*, *14*, 341–367.

Burr, V. (1998). *Gender and social psychology*. London: Routledge.

Cabeza, R., Mangels, J., Nyberg, L., Habib, R., Houle, S., McIntosh, A. R., & Tulving, E. (1997). Brain regions differentially involved in remembering what and when: A PET study. *Neuro*, *19*, 863–870.

Calamandrei, G., Alleva, E., Cirulli, F., Queyras, A., Volterra, V., Capirci, O., Vicari, S., Giannotti, A., Turrini, P., & Aloe, L. (2000). Serum NGF levels in children and adolescents with either Williams syndrome or Down syndrome. *Developmental Medicine and Child Neurology*, *42*, 746–750.

Caltagirone, C., Nocentini, U., & Vicari, S. (1990). Cognitive functions in adult Down's syndrome. *International Journal of Neuroscience*, *54*, 221–230.

Caplan, P. J., Crawford, M., Hyde, J. S., & Richardson, J. T. E. (1997). *Gender differences in human cognition*. New York: Oxford University Press.

Carlesimo, G. A., Marotta, L., & Vicari, S. (1996). Long-term memory in mental retardation:

Evidence for a specific impairment in subjects with Down's syndrome. *Neuropsychologia, 35,* 71–79.

Carlesimo, G. A., Perri, R., Turriziani, P., Tomaiuolo, F., & Caltagirone, C. (2001). Remembering what but not where: Independence of spatial and visual working memory in the human brain. *Cortex, 37,* 519–537.

Carpenter, P. A., & Eisenberg, P. (1978). Mental rotation and the frame of reference in blind and sighted individuals. *Perception and Psychophysics, 23,* 117–124.

Carreiras, M., & Codina, M. (1992). Spatial cognition of the blind and sighted: Visual and amodal hypotheses. *Cahiers de Psychologie Cognitive, 12,* 51–78.

Carroll, J. B. (1993). *Human cognitive abilities: A survey of factor-analytic studies.* New York: Cambridge University Press.

Carter, C. H. (1979). *Handbook of mental retardation syndromes.* Springfield, IL: Thomas.

Case, R. (1985). *Intellectual development: Birth to adulthood.* London: Academic Press.

Caselli, M. C., Vicari, S., Longobardi, E., Lami, L., Pizzoli, C., & Stella, G. (1998). Gestures and words in early development of children with Down syndrome. *Journal of Speech Language and Hearing Research, 41,* 1125–1135.

Casey, M. B. (1996). Understanding individual differences in spatial ability within females: A nature/nurture interactionist framework. *Developmental Review, 16,* 241–260.

Cerella, J. (1990). Aging and information processing rate. In J. E. Birren & K. W. Schaie (Eds.), *Handbook of the psychology of aging* (3rd ed., pp. 201–221). San Diego, CA: Academic Press.

Cerella, J. (1991). Age effects may be global, not local: Comment on Fisk and Rogers (1991). *Journal of Experimental Psychology: General, 120,* 215–223.

Cermak, L. S. (1993). Automatic vs. controlled processing and the implicit task performance of amnesic patients. In P. Graf & M. E. J. Masson (Eds.), *Implicit memory, new directions in cognition, development and neuropsychology* (pp. 287–302). Hillsdale, NJ: Lawrence Erlbaum Associates Inc.

Chambers, D., & Reisberg, D. (1985). Can mental images be ambiguous? *Journal of Experimental Psychology: Human Perception and Performance, 11,* 317–328.

Chieffi, S., & Allport, D. A. (1997). Independent coding of target distance and direction in visuo-spatial working memory. *Psychological Research, 60,* 244–250.

Christensen, H., Mackinnon, A. J., Korten, A. E., Jorm, A. F., Henderson, A. S., Jacomb, P., & Rodgers, B. (1999). An analysis of diversity in the cognitive performance of elderly community dwellers: Individual differences in change scores as a function of age. *Psychology and Aging, 14,* 365–379.

Chuah, Y. M. L., & Maybery, M. T. (1999). Verbal and spatial short-term memory: Common sources of developmental change? *Journal of Experimental Child Psychology, 73,* 7–44.

Cohen, D., Schaie, K. W., & Gribbin, K. (1977) The organisation of spatial abilities in older men and women. *Journal of Gerontology, 32,* 578–585.

Cohen, J. (1969). *Statistical power analysis for the behavioral sciences* (rev. ed.). New York: Academic Press.

Colon, R., Quiroga, M. A., & Juan-Espinosa, M. (1999). Are cognitive sex differences disappearing? Evidence from Spanish population. *Personality and Individual Differences, 27,* 1189–1195.

Conte, A., & Cornoldi, C. (1997). Il contributo della memoria visuospaziale alle attivita' della vita quotidiana. In L. Czerwinsky Domenis (Ed.), *Obiettivo bambino. Dalla ricerca pura alla ricerca applicata* (pp. 157–166). Milano: Angeli.

Conte, A., Cornoldi, C., Pazzaglia, F., & Sanavio, S. (1995). The development of the visuo-spatial working memory and its role in spatial memory. *Ricerche di Psicologia, 19,* 95–114.

Cooper, D. N., & Hall, C. (1988). Down's syndrome and the molecular biology of chromosome 21. *Progress in Neurobiology, 30,* 507–530.

Corballis, M. C., & Beale, I. L. (1976). *The psychology of left and right*. Hillsdale, NJ: Lawrence Erlbaum Associates Inc.

Cornell, E. H., Heth, C. D., & Alberts, D. M. (1994). Place recognition and way finding by children and adults. *Memory and Cognition, 22*, 633–643.

Cornish, K. M., Munir, F., & Cross, G. (1998). The nature of the spatial deficit in young females with fragile-X syndrome: A neuropsychological and molecular perspective. *Neuropsychologia, 36*, 1239–1246.

Cornoldi, C. (1975). *L'esame della memoria*. Padova, Italy: CLEUP.

Cornoldi, C. (1995). La memoria di lavoro visuo-spaziale. In F. S. Marucci (Ed.), *Le immagini mentali* (pp. 145–181). Roma: Nuova Italia Scientifica.

Cornoldi, C., Bertuccelli, B., Rocchi, P., & Sbrana, B. (1993). Processing capacity limitations in pictorial and spatial representations in the totally congenitally blind. *Cortex, 29*, 675–689.

Cornoldi, C., Braga, C., & Mammarella, N. (2002a). *Visuo-spatial working memory and interference control in children with visuo-spatial deficits*. Manuscript in preparation.

Cornoldi, C., Calore, D., & Pra Baldi, A. (1979). Imagery ratings and recall in congenitally blind subjects. *Perceptual and Motor Skills, 48*, 627–629.

Cornoldi, C., Carretti, B., & De Beni, R. (2001b). How the pattern of deficits in groups of learning-disabled individuals help to understand the organisation of working memory. *Issues in Education, 7*, 71–78.

Cornoldi, C., Cortesi, A., & Preti, D. (1991b). Individual differences in the capacity limitations of visuospatial short-term memory: Research on sighted and totally congenitally blind people. *Memory and Cognition, 19*, 459–468.

Cornoldi, C., Dalla Vecchia, R., & Tressoldi, P. E. (1995). Visuo-spatial working memory limitations in low visuo-spatial high verbal intelligence children. *Journal of Child Psychology and Psychiatry, 36*, 1053–1064.

Cornoldi, C., & De Beni, R., (1988). Weakness of imagery without visual experience: The case of the total congenital blind using imaginal mnemonics. In M. Denis, J. Engelkamp, & J. T. E. Richardson (Eds.), *Cognitive and neuropsychological approaches to mental imagery* (pp. 393–401). Dordrecht, Netherlands: Nijhoff.

Cornoldi, C., De Beni, R., Giusberti, F., Marucci, F. S., Massironi, M., & Mazzoni, G. (1991a). The study of vividness of images. In R. H. Logie & M. Denis (Eds.), *Mental images in human cognition* (pp. 305–312). Amsterdam: North-Holland, Elsevier.

Cornoldi, C., De Beni, R., Giusberti, F., & Massironi, M. (1998). Memory and imagery: A visual trace is not a mental image. In M. A. Conway, S. E. Gathercole, & C. Cornoldi (Eds.), Theories of memory (Vol. II, pp. 87–110). Hove, UK: Psychology Press.

Cornoldi, C., De Beni, R., & Pazzaglia, F. (1996b). Profiles of reading comprehension difficulties: An analysis of single cases. In C. Cornoldi & J. Oakhill (Eds.), *Reading comprehension difficulties: Processesd intervention* (pp. 113–136). Hillsdale, NJ: Lawrence Erlbaum Associates Inc.

Cornoldi, C., De Beni, R., Roncari, S., & Romano, S. (1989). The effects of imagery instructions on totally congenitally blind recall. *European Journal of Cognitive Psychology, 1*, 321–331.

Cornoldi, C., Friso, G., Giordano, L., Molin, A., Poli, S., Rigoni, F., & Tressoldi, P. E. (1997). *Abilità visuo-spaziali*. Trento, Italy: Erickson.

Cornoldi, C., & Guglielmo, A. (2001). Children who cannot imagine. *Korean Journal of Thinking & Problem Solving, 11*, 99–112.

Cornoldi, C., Logie, R. H., Brandimonte, M. A., Kaufmann, G., & Reisberg, D. (1996a). *Stretching the imagination: Representation and transformation in mental imagery*. New York: Oxford University Press.

Cornoldi, C., & Mammarella, N. (submitted). Intrusion errors in visuospatial working memory. *Memory*.

Cornoldi, C., Marconi, F., & Vecchi, T. (2001a). Visuospatial working memory in Turner's syndrome. *Brain and Cognition, 46*, 90–94.

Cornoldi, C., Marzocchi, G. M., Belotti, M., Caroli, M. G., De Meo, T., & Braga, C. (in press). Working memory interference control deficit in children referred by teachers for ADHD symptoms. *Child Neuropsychology*.

Cornoldi, C., Rigoni, F., Tressoldi, P. E., & Vio, C. (1999). Imagery deficits in nonverbal learning disabilities. *Journal of Learning Disabilities, 32*, 48–57.

Cornoldi, C., Rigoni, F., Venneri, A., & Vecchi, T. (2000). Passive and active processes in visuo-spatial memory: Double dissociation in developmental learning disabilities. *Brain and Cognition, 43*, 17–20.

Cornoldi, C., Tinti, C., & Vecchi, T. (2002b). *Memory and integration processes in congenital blindness*. Manuscript in preparation.

Cornoldi, C., & Vecchi, T. (2000). Mental imagery in blind people: The role of passive and active visuo-spatial processes. In M. Heller (Ed.), *Touch, representation, and blindness* (pp. 143–181). Oxford: Oxford University Press.

Corsi, P. M. (1972). *Human memory and the medial temporal region of the brain*. Doctoral dissertation, McGill University, Montreal.

Courtney, S. M., Petit, L., Maisog, J. Ma., Ungerleider, L. G., & Haxby, J. V. (1998). An area specialized for spatial working memory in human frontal cortex. *Science, 279*, 1347–1351.

Courtney, S. M., Ungerleider, L. G., Keil, K., & Haxby, J. V. (1996). Object and spatial working memory activate separate neural systems in human cortex. *Cerebral Cortex, 6*, 39–49.

Cowan, N. (1988). Evolving conceptions of memory storage, selective attention, and their mutual constraints within the human information processing system. *Psychological Bulletin, 104*, 163–191.

Cowan, N. (1995). *Attention and memory: An integrated framework*. New York: Oxford University Press.

Craik, F. I. M., & Jennings, J. M. (1992). Human memory. In F. I. M. Craik & T. A. Salthouse (Eds.), *The handbook of aging and cognition* (pp. 51–110). Hillsdale, NJ: Lawrence Erlbaum Associates Inc.

Craik, F. I. M., & Salthouse, T. A. (Eds.) (1992). *The handbook of aging and cognition*. Hillsdale, NJ: Lawrence Erlbaum Associates Inc.

Craik, F. I. M., & Salthouse, T. A. (Eds.) (2000). *The handbook of aging and cognition* (2nd ed.). Hillsdale, NJ: Lawrence Erlbaum Associates Inc.

Crowe, S. F., & Hay, A. (1990). Neuropsychological dimensions of the fragile X syndrome: Support for a non-dominant hemisphere dysfunction hypothesis. *Neuropsychologia, 28*, 9–16.

Daneman, M., & Carpenter, P. A. (1980). Individual differences in working memory and reading. *Journal of Verbal Learning and Verbal Behavior, 19*, 450–466.

Daneman, M., & Tardif, T. (1987). Working memory and reading skill re-examined. In M. Coltheart (Ed.), *Attention and performance XII* (pp. 491–508). Hillsdale, NJ: Lawrence Erlbaum Associates Inc.

Davidoff, J. (1991). *Cognition through color*. Cambridge, MA: MIT Press.

Davidoff, J. (1997). The neuropsychology of color. In C. L. Hardin & L. Maffi (Eds.), *Color categories in thought and language* (pp. 118–134). New York: Cambridge University Press.

Dawson, J. L. M. (1972). Effects of sex hormones on cognitive style in rats and men. *Behavior Genetics, 2*, 21–42.

De Beni, R., & Cornoldi, C. (1985a). The effects of imaginal mnemonics on congenitally totally blind and on normal subjects. In D. F. Marks & D. G. Russel (Eds.), *Imagery I*. Dunedin, New Zealand: Human Performance Associates.

De Beni, R., & Cornoldi, C. (1985b). Effects of the mnemotechnique of loci in the memorization of concrete words. *Acta Psychologica, 60*, 11–24.

De Beni, R., & Cornoldi, C. (1988). Imagery limitations in totally congenitally blind subjects. *Journal of Experimental Psychology: Learning, Memory and Cognition, 14*, 650–655.

De Beni, R., Palladino, P., Pazzaglia, F., & Cornoldi, C. (1998). Increases in intrusion errors and working memory deficit of poor comprehenders. *Quarterly Journal of Experimental Psychology*, *51A*, 305–320.

Della Sala, S., Gray, C., Baddeley, A., Allamano, N., & Wilson, L. (1999). Pattern span: A tool for unwelding visuo-spatial memory. *Neuropsychologia*, *37*, 1189–1199.

Della Sala, S., Gray, C., Baddeley, A. D., & Wilson, L. (1997). *Visual Pattern Test*. Bury St Edmunds, UK: Thames Valley Test Company.

DeLoache, J. S., & Brown, A. L. (1983). Very young children's memory for location of objects in a large-scale environment. *Child Development*, *54*, 888–897.

Dempster, F. N. (1993). Resistance to interference: Toward a unified theory of cognitive development and aging. *Developmental Review*, *12*, 45–75.

Denes, G., & Pizzamiglio, L. (Eds.) (1999). *Handbook of clinical and experimental neuropsychology*. Hove, UK: Psychology Press.

Denis, M., Daniel, M. P., Fontaine, S., & Pazzaglia, F. (2001b). Language, spatial cognition, and navigation. In M. Denis, R. H. Logie, C. Cornoldi, M. de Vega, & J. Engelkamp (Eds.), *Imagery, language and visuo-spatial thinking* (pp. 137–160). Hove, UK: Psychology Press.

Denis, M., & Kosslyn, S. M. (1999). Scanning visual mental images: A window on the mind. *Cahiers de Psychologie Cognitive*, *18*, 409–465.

Denis, M., Logie, R. H., Cornoldi, C., De Vega, M., & Engelkamp, J. (Eds.) (2001a). *Imagery, language and visuo-spatial thinking*. Hove, UK: Psychology Press.

De Renzi, E. (1982). *Disorders of space exploration and cognition*. New York: John Wiley.

De Renzi, E., & Nichelli, P. (1975). Verbal and non-verbal short-term memory impairment following hemispheric damage. *Cortex*, *11*, 341–354.

De Ribaupierre, A., & Ludwig, C. (2000). Attention divisée et vielissement cognitif: Différences d'age dans 5 épreuves duelles de memorie de travail. In D. Brouillet (Ed.), *Le vielissement cogniitf normal. Vers un modèle explicatif du vielissement* (pp. 29–51). Brussels, Belgium: DeBoeck.

Dixon, R. A., & Hertzog, C. (1996). Theoretical issues in cognition and aging. In F. Blanchard-Fields & T. M. Hess (Eds.), *Perspectives on cognitive change in adulthood and aging* (pp. 25–65). New York: McGraw-Hill.

Down, J. L. H. (1866). Observation on an ethnic classification of idiots. *London Hospital Clinical Lectures and Reports*, *3*, 259.

Down, J. L. H. (1887). *On some of the mental afflictions of childhood and youth*. London: Churchill.

Dror, I. E., & Kosslyn, S. M. (1994). Mental imagery and aging. *Psychology and Aging*, *9*, 90–102.

Duff, S. C., & Logie, R. H. (2001). Processing and storage in working memory span. *Quarterly Journal of Experimental Psychology*, *54A*, 31–48.

Easton, R. D., Srinivas, K., & Greene, A. J. (1997). Do vision and haptics share common representations—Implicit and explicit memory within and between modalities. *Journal of Experimental Psychology: Learning, Memory and Cognition*, *23*, 153–163.

Ehrlich, M. F., Brebion, J., & Tardieu, H. (1994). Working-memory capacity and reading comprehension in young and older adults. *Psychological Research*, *56*, 110–115.

Eilan, N. (1993). Introduction: Intuitive physics. In N. Eilan, R. McCarthy, & B. Brewer (Eds.), *Spatial representation* (pp. 99–111). Oxford: Blackwell.

Elithorn, A., Jones, D., Kerr, M., & Lee, D. (1964). The effects of the variation of two physical parameters on empirical difficulty in a perceptual maze test. *British Journal of Psychology*, *55*, 31–37.

Engelkamp, J., Zimmer, H. D., & de Vega, M. (2001). Pictures in memory: The role of visual–imaginal information. In M. Denis, R. H. Logie, C. Cornoldi, M. de Vega, & J. Engelkamp (Eds.), *Imagery, language and visuo-spatial thinking* (pp. 59–80). Hove, UK: Psychology Press.

Engle, R. W., Kane, M. J., & Tuholski, S. W. (1999a). Individual differences in working memory capacity and what they tell us about controlled attention, general fluid intelligence, and functions of the prefrontal cortex. In A. Miyake & P. Shah (Eds.), *Models of working memory* (pp. 102–134). Cambridge: Cambridge University Press.

Engle, R. W., Tuholski, S. W., Laughlin, J. E., & Conway, A. R. A. (1999b). Working memory, short-term memory, and general fluid intelligence: A latent-variable approach. *Journal of Experimental Psychology: General, 128,* 309–331.

Ericsson, K. A., & Kintsch, W. (1995). Long-term working memory. *Psychological Review, 102,* 211–245.

Eslinger, P. J., Biddle, K., Pennington, B., & Page, R. B. (1999). Cognitive and behavioral development up to 4 years after early right frontal lobe lesion. *Developmental Neuropsychology, 15,* 157–191.

Ewart, A., Morris, C. A., Atkinson, D., Jin, W., Sternes, K., Spallone, P., Stock, D., Leppert, M., & Keating, M. T. (1993). Hemizygosity at the elastin locus in a developmental disorder: Williams syndrome. *Nature Genetics, 5,* 11–16.

Fabbretti, D., Pizzuto, E., Vicari, S., & Volterra, V. (1997). A story description task in children with Down's syndrome: Lexical and morphosyntactic abilities. *Journal of Intellectual Disability Research, 41,* 165–179.

Fagan, J. F. (1970). Memory in the infant. *Journal of Experimental Child Psychology, 9,* 217–226.

Fahle, M., & Daum, I. (1997). Visual learning and memory as functions of age. *Neuropsychologia, 35,* 1583–1589.

Farah, M. J. (1984). The neurological basis of mental imagery: A componential analysis. *Cognition, 18,* 245–272.

Farah, M. J., Hammond, K. M., Levine, D. N., & Calvanio, R. (1988). Visual and spatial mental imagery: Dissociable systems of representation. *Cognitive Psychology, 20,* 439–462.

Fastame, M. C., Cornoldi, C., & Vecchi, T. (2001). Working memory and drawing: A developmental perspective. *Abstract of the 8th EWIC-European Workshop on Imagery and Cognition* (p. 50), Saint-Malo, France, April 1–3.

Feingold, A. (1988). Cognitive gender differences are disappearing. *American Psychologist, 43,* 95–103.

Ferrer, L., & Gullotta, F. (1990). Down's syndrome and Alzheimer's disease: Dendritic spine counts in the hippocampus. *Acta Neuropathologica, 79,* 680–685.

Finke, R. A., & Slayton, K. (1988). Explorations of creative visual synthesis in mental imagery. *Memory and Cognition, 16,* 252–257.

Fleming, K., Goldberg, T. E., Binks, S., & Randolph, C. (1997). Visuospatial working memory in patients with schizophrenia. *Biological Psychiatry, 41,* 43–49.

Fodor, J. A. (1983). *The modularity of mind.* Cambridge, MA: MIT Press

Foreman, N., & Gillet, R. (Eds.) (1997). *Handbook of spatial research paradigms and methodologies* (Vol. 1). Hove, UK: Psychology Press.

Foreman, N., Warry, R., & Murray, P. (1990). Development of reference and working spatial memory in preschool children. *Journal of General Psychology, 117,* 267–276.

Freund, L. S., & Reiss, A. L. (1991). Cognitive profiles associated with the fragile X syndrome in males and females. *American Journal of Medical Genetics, 38,* 83–98.

Friedman, N. P., & Miyake, A. (2000). Differential roles for visuospatial and verbal working memory in situation model construction. *Journal of Experimental Psychology: General, 129,* 61–83.

Frieske, D. A., & Park, D. C. (1999). Memory for news in young and old people. *Psychology and Aging, 14,* 90–98.

Frigotto, D. S., & Cornoldi, C. (2001). The effects of a "Relaxation Visualization Condition" on a creative mental synthesis task. *Abstract of the 8th EWIC European Workshop on Imagery and Cognition* (p. 52), Saint-Malo, France, April 1–3.

Galton, F. (1883). *Enquiries into human faculty and its development.* London: Macmillan.

Garden, S., Cornoldi, C., & Logie, R. H. (2001). Visuo-spatial working memory in navigation. *Applied Cognitive Psychology, 16*, 35–50.

Gathercole, S. E., & Pickering, S. J. (2000). Working memory deficits in children with low achievements in the national curriculum at 7 years of age. *British Journal of Educational Psychology, 70*, 177–194.

Gaylord, S. A., & Marsh, G. R. (1975). Age differences in the speed of a spatial cognitive process. *Journal of Gerontology, 30*, 674–678.

Gick, M. L., Craik, F. I. M., & Morris, M. G. (1988). Task complexity and age differences in working memory. *Memory and Cognition, 16*, 353–361.

Giusberti, F., Cornoldi, C., De Beni, R., & Massironi, M. (1992). Differences in vividness ratings of perceived and imagined patterns. *British Journal of Psychology, 83*, 533–547.

Giusberti, F., Cornoldi, C., De Beni, R., & Massironi, M. (1998). Perceptual illusions in imagery. *European Psychologist, 3*, 281–288.

Goldman-Rakic, P. S. (1987). Circuit basis of a cognitive function in non-human primates. In S. M. Stahl & S. D. Iversen (Eds.), *Cognitive neurochemistry* (pp. 90–110). New York: Oxford University Press.

Goodale, M. A., Meenan, J. P., Bulthoff, H. H., Nicolle, D. A., Murphy, K. J., & Racicot, C. I. (1994). Separate neural pathways for the visual analysis of object shape in perception and prehension. *Current Biology, 4*, 604–610.

Goodale, M. A., & Milner, A. D. (1992). Separate visual pathways for perception and action. *Trends in Neurosciences, 15*, 20–25.

Grant, J., Karmiloff-Smith, A., Gathercole, S. A., Paterson, S., Howlin, P., Davies, M., & Udwin, O. (1997). Phonological short-term memory and its relationship to language in Williams syndrome. *Cognitive Neuropsychiatry, 2*, 81–99.

Grossi, D., Orsini, A., Modafferi, A., & Listti, M. (1986). Visuoimaginal constructional apraxia: On a case of selective deficit of imagery. *Brain and Cognition, 5*, 255–267.

Gyselinck, V., Ehrlich, M. F., Cornoldi, C., De Beni, R., & Dubois, V. (2000). Visuospatial working memory in learning from multimedia systems. *Journal of Computer Assisted Learning, 16*, 166–176.

Hagerman, R. J., & Cronister, A. (1996). *Fragile X syndrome: Diagnosis, treatment and research* (2nd ed.). Baltimore, MD: Johns Hopkins University Press.

Haller, J. S. Jr., & Haller, R. M. (1974). *The physician and sexuality in Victorian America*. Urbana, IL: University of Illinois Press.

Halpern, D. F. (2000). *Sex differences in cognitive abilities* (3rd ed.). Mahwah, NJ: Lawrence Erlbaum Associates Inc.

Hampson, R. E., Simeral, J. D., & Deadwyler, S. A. (1999). Distribution of spatial and non-spatial information in dorsal hippocampus. *Nature, 402*, 810–814.

Hanley, J. R., Young, A. W., & Pearson, N. A. (1991). Impairment of the visuo-spatial sketch pad. *Quarterly Journal of Experimental Psychology, 43A*, 101–125.

Harshman, R. A., Hampson, E., & Berenbaum, S. A. (1983) Individual differences in cognitive abilities and brain organization, Part 1: Sex and handedness differences in ability. *Canadian Journal of Psychology, 37*, 144–192.

Harshman, R. A., & Paivio, A. (1987) "Paradoxical" sex differences in self-reported imagery. *Canadian Journal of Psychology, 41*, 287–302.

Hartman, M., & Potter, G. (1998). Sources of age differences on the Rey–Osterrieth Complex Figure Test. *Clinical Neuropsychologist, 12*, 513–524.

Hasher, L., & Zacks, R. T. (1979). Automatic and effortful processes in memory. *Journal of Experimental Psychology: General, 108*, 356–388.

Hasher, L., & Zacks, R. T. (1988). Working memory, comprehension, and aging: A review and a new view. In G. H. Bower (Ed); *The psychology of learning and motivation: Advances in research and theory*. San Diego, CA: Academic Press.

Haug, H. (1987). Brain sizes, surface, and neuronal sizes of the cortex cerebri: A stereological investigation of man and his variability and a comparison with some species of mammals (primates, whales, marsupials, insectivores, and one elephant). *Americal Journal of Anatomy, 180*, 126–142.

Haugeland, J. (Ed.) (1997). *Mind design 2: Philosophy, psychology, artificial intelligence* (Rev. & enlarged 2nd ed.). Cambridge, MA: MIT Press.

Haxby, J. V., Grady, C. L., Horwitz, B., Ungerleider, L. G., Mishkin, M., Carson, R. E., Herscovitch, P., Shapiro, M. B., & Rapaport, S. I. (1991). Dissociation of object and spatial vision processing pathways in human extrastriate cortex. *Neurobiology, 88*, 1621–1625.

Hecker, R., & Mapperson, B. (1997). Dissociation of visual and spatial processing in working memory. *Neuropsychologia, 35*, 599–603.

Hedges, L. V., & Nowell, A. (1995). Sex differences in mental test scores, variability, and numbers of high-scoring individuals. *Science, 269*, 41–45.

Heller, M. A., Calcaterra, J. A., Green, S., & Lima, F. (1999). The effect of orientation on braille recognition in persons who are sighted and blind. *Journal of Visual Impairment and Blindness, 93*, 416–419.

Heller, M. A., Calcaterra, J. A., Tyler, L. A., & Burson, L. L. (1996). Production and interpretation of perspective drawings by blind and sighted people. *Perception, 25*, 321–334.

Hertzog, C., & Rypma, B. (1991). Age differences in components of mental-rotation task performance. *Bulletin of the Psychonomic Society, 29*, 209–212.

Hitch, G. J., Brandimonte, M. A., & Walker, P. (1995). Two types of representation in visual memory: Evidence from the effects of stimulus contrast on image combination. *Memory and Cognition, 23*, 147–154.

Hitch, G. J., Halliday, M. S., Schaafstal, A. M., & Heffernan, T. M. (1991). Speech, "inner speech", and the development of short-term memory: Effects of picture-labeling on recall. *Journal of Experimental Child Psychology, 51*, 220–234.

Hitch, G. J., Halliday, M. S., Schaafstal, A. M., & Schraagen, J. M. C. (1988). Visual working memory in young children. *Memory and Cognition, 16*, 120–132.

Hitch, G., Towse, J. N., & Hutton, U. (2001). What limits children's working memory span? Theoretical accounts and applications for scholastic development. *Journal of Experimental Psychology: General, 130*, 184–198.

Hooper, H. E. (1958). *The Hooper Visual Organization Test. Manual.* Los Angeles: Western Psychological Series.

Hulme, C., & Mackenzie, S. (1992). *Working memory and severe learning difficulties.* Hillsdale, NJ: Lawrence Erlbaum Associates Inc.

Hultsch, D. F., Hertzog, C., Small, B. J., & Dixon, R. A. (1999). Use it or lose it: Engaged lifestyle as a buffer of cognitive decline in aging? *Psychology and Aging, 14*, 245–263.

Hyde, J. S. (1981). How large are cognitive gender differences? *Developmental Psychology, 20*, 722–736.

Hyde, J. S., Fennema, E., & Lamon, S. J. (1990). Gender differences in mathematics performance: A meta-analysis. *Psychological Bulletin, 107*, 139–155.

Hyde, J. S., & Linn, M. C. (1988). Gender differences in verbal ability: A meta-analysis. *Psychological Bulletin, 104*, 53–69.

Hyde, J. S., & McKinley, N. M. (1997). Gender differences in cognition: Results from meta-analyses. In P. J. Caplan, M. Crawford, J. S. Hyde, & J. T. E. Richardson (Eds.), *Gender differences in human cognition* (pp. 30–51). New York: Oxford University Press.

Intons-Peterson, M. J. (1996). Integrating the components of imagery. In M. de Vega, M. J. Intons-Peterson, P. N. Johnson-Laird, M. Denis, & M. Marschark (Eds.), *Models of visuo-spatial cognition* (pp. 20–89). New York: Oxford University Press.

Jakala, P., Hanninen, T., Ryynaum, M., Laakso, M., Partanen, K., Mannermaa, A., & Soinen,

H. (1997). Fragile X: Neuropsychological test performance, CGG triplets repeat lengths, and hippocampal volumes. *Journal of Clinical Investigation, 100*, 331–338.

Jarrold, C., Baddeley, A. D., & Hewes, A. K. (1998). Verbal and nonverbal abilities in the Williams syndrome phenotype: Evidence for diverging developmental trajectories. *Journal of Child Psychology and Psychiatry, 39*, 511–523.

Jarrold, C., Baddeley, A. D., & Hewes, A. K. (1999). Genetically dissociated components of working memory: Evidence from Down's and Williams syndrome. *Neuropsychologia, 37*, 637–651.

Jenkins, L. Myerson, J., Hale, S., & Fry, A. F. (2000b). Individual and developmental differences in working memory across the life span. *Psychonomic Bulletin and Review, 6*, 28–40.

Jenkins, L., Myerson, J., Joerding, J. A., & Hale, S. (2000a). Converging evidence that visuospatial cognition is more age-sensitive than verbal cognition. *Psychology and Aging, 15*, 157–175.

Jensen, A. R. (1988). Sex differences in arithmetic computation and reasoning in prepubertal boys and girls. *Behavioral and Brain Sciences, 11*, 198–199.

Jernigan, T. L., Bellugi, U., Sowell, E., Doherty, S., & Hesselink, J. R. (1993). Cerebral morphological distinction between Williams and Down syndromes. *Archives of Neurology, 50*, 186–191.

Jiang, Y., Olson, I. R., & Chun, M. M. (2000). Organization of visual short-term memory. *Journal of Experimental Psychology: Learning, Memory and Cognition, 26*, 683–702.

Johnson, E. S., & Meade, A. C. (1987). Developmental patterns of spatial ability: An early sex difference. *Child Development, 58*, 725–740.

Johnson, P. (1982). The functional equivalence of imagery and movement. *Quarterly Journal of Experimental Psychology, 34A*, 349–365.

Jones, K. L., & Smith, D. W. (1995). The Williams elfin faces syndrome: A new perspective. *Journal of Pediatrics, 86*, 718–723.

Jonides, J., Kahn, R., & Rozin, P. (1975). Imagery instructions improve memory in blind subjects. *Bulletin of the Psychonomic Society, 5*, 424–426.

Jonides, J., Smith, E. E., Koeppe, R. A., & Awh, E. (1993). Spatial working memory in humans as revealed by PET. *Nature, 363*, 623–625.

Just, M. A., & Carpenter, P. A. (1992). A capacity theory of comprehension: Individual differences in working memory. *Psychological Review, 99*, 122–149.

Just, M. A., Carpenter, P. A., Maguire, M., Diwadkar, V., & McMains, S. (2001). Mental rotation of objects retrieved from memory: A functional MRI study of spatial processing. *Journal of Experimental Psychology: General, 130*, 493–504.

Juurmaa, J., & Lehtinen-Railo, S. (1994). Visual experience and access to spatial knowledge. *Journal of Visual Impairment and Blindness, 88*, 157–170.

Kail, R. (1988). "Developmental changes in speed of processing: Central limiting mechanism or skill transfer?": Reply to Stigler, Nusbaum, and Chalip. *Child Development, 59*, 1154–1157.

Kail, R., Carter, P., & Pellegrino, J. (1979). The locus of sex differences in spatial ability. *Perception and Psychophysics, 26*, 213–217.

Kane, M., Bleckley, M. K., Conway, A. R. A., & Engle, R. (2001). A controlled-attention view of working memory capacity. *Journal of Experimental Psychology: General, 130*, 169–183.

Katz, E. R., & Ellis, N. R. (1991). Memory for spatial location in retarded and nonretarded persons. *Journal of Mental Deficiency Research, 35*, 209–220.

Kaufman, A. S., & Doppelt, J. E. (1977). Analysis of WISC-R standardization in terms of the stratifications variables. *Child Development, 47*, 165–171.

Kazdin, A. E., & Kagan, J. (1994). Models of dysfunction in developmental psychopathology. *Clinical Psychology: Science and Practice, 1*, 35–52.

Kemps, E. (1999). Effects of complexity on visuo-spatial working memory. *European Journal of Cognitive Psychology, 11*, 335–356.

Kennedy, J. (1982). Haptic pictures. In W. Schiff & E. Foulke (Eds.), *Tactual perception*. New York: Academic Press.

Kennedy, J. (1993). *Drawing and the blind: Pictures to touch*. New Haven, CT: Yale University Press.

Kerr, N. H. (1983). The role of vision in visual imagery experiments: Evidence from the congenitally blind. *Journal of Experimental Psychology: General, 112*, 265–277.

Kerr, N. H. (1987). Locational representation in imagery: The third dimension. *Memory and Cognition, 15*, 521–530.

Kerr, N. H. (1993). Rate of imagery processing in two versus three dimensions. *Memory and Cognition, 21*, 467–476.

Kessels, R. P. C., Postma, A., & De Haan, E. H. F. (1999). Object relocation: A program for setting up, running, and analyzing experiments on memory for object locations. *Behavior Research Methods, Instruments and Computers, 31*, 423–428.

Kessels, R. P. C., van Zandvoort, M. J. E., Postma, A., Kappelle, L. J., & de Haan, E. H. F. (2000). The Corsi Block-Tapping task: Standardization and normative data. *Applied Neuropsychology, 7*, 252–258.

Kimura, D. (1999). *Sex and cognition*. Cambridge, MA: MIT Press.

Klatzky, R. L., Golledge, R. G., Loomis, J. M., Cicinelli, J. G., & Pellegrino, J. W. (1995). Performance of blind and sighted persons on spatial tasks. *Journal of Visual Impairment and Blindness, 91*, 70–82.

Klein, B. P., & Mervis, C. B. (1999). Contrasting patterns of cognitive abilities of 9- and 10-year-olds with Williams syndrome or Down syndrome. *Developmental Neuropsychology, 16*, 177–196.

Kosslyn, S. M. (1973). Scanning visual images: Some structural implications. *Perception and Psychophysics, 14*, 90–94.

Kosslyn, S. M. (1980). *Image and mind*. Cambridge, MA: Harvard University Press.

Kosslyn, S. M. (1994). *Image and brain*. Cambridge, MA: MIT Press.

Kosslyn, S. M., Ball, T. M., & Rieser, B. J. (1978). Visual images preserve metric spatial information: Evidence from studies of image scanning. *Journal of Experimental Psychology: Human Perception and Performance, 4*, 47–60.

Kosslyn, S. M., Brunn, J., Cave, K. R., & Wallach, R. W. (1984). Individual differences in mental imagery ability: A computational analysis. *Cognition, 18*, 195–243.

Kosslyn, S. M., Margolis, J. A., Barrett, A. M., Goldknopf, E. J., & Caly, P. F. (1990b). Age differences in imagery disabilities. *Child Development, 61*, 995–1010.

Kosslyn, S. M., Van Kleeck, M. H., & Kirby, K. N. (1990a). A neurologically plausible model of individual differences in visual mental imagery. In P. J. Hampson, D. F. Marks, & J. T. E. Richardson (Eds.), *Imagery: Current developments* (pp. 39–77). London: Routledge.

Kroll, N. E. A. (1975). Visual short-term memory. In D. Deutsch & J. A. Deutsch (Eds.), *Short term memory* (pp. 153–179). New York: Academic Press.

Lanfranchi, S., Cornoldi, C., & Vianello, R. (2002a). *Working memory deficits in children with Down syndrome*. Paper presented at the fourth European meeting on mental retardation, Catania, Italy, May 23–25.

Lanfranchi, S., Cornoldi, C., & Vianello, R. (2002b). *Working memory deficits in individuals with and without mental retardation*. Manuscript submitted for publication.

Lange-Kuettner, C., & Friederici, A. D. (2000). Modularity of object and place memory in children. *Learning Disabilities, 32*, 48–57.

Law, D. J., Pellegrino, J. W., & Hunt, E. B. (1993). Comparing the tortoise and the hare: Gender differences and experience in dynamic spatial reasoning tasks. *Psychological Science, 4*, 35–40.

Lawrence, B. M., Myerson, J., Oonk, H. M., & Abrams, R. A. (2001). The effects of eye and limb movements on working memory. *Memory, 9*, 433–444.

Lawton, C. A., & Morrin, K. A. (1999). Gender differences in pointing accuracy in computer-simulated 3D mazes. *Sex Roles, 40*, 73–92.

Lee, D., & Chun, M. M. (2001). What are the units of visual short-term memory, objects or spatial locations? *Perception and Psychophysics*, *63*, 253–257.

Lejeune, M. (1994). Role of proximity and spatial position of stimulus characteristics during the development of mental rotation capacities. *Cahiers de Psychologie Cognitive*, *13*, 469–492.

Levine, D. N., Warach, J., & Farah, M. J. (1984). Two visual systems in mental imagery: Dissociation of "what" and "where" in imagery disorders due to bilateral posterior cerebral lesions. *Neurology*, *35*, 1010–1018.

Levine, S. C., Huttenlocher, J., Taylor, A., & Langrock, A. (1999). Early sex differences in spatial skill. *Developmental Psychology*, *35*, 940–949.

Light, L. L., & La Voie, D. (1993). Direct and indirect measures of memory in old age. In P. Graf & M. E. J. Masson (Eds.), *Implicit memory, new directions in cognition, development and neuropsychology* (pp. 207–230). Hillsdale, NJ: Lawrence Erlbaum Associates Inc.

Lindenberger, U., Marsiske, M., & Baltes, P. B. (2000). Memorizing while walking: Increase in dual-task costs from young adulthood to old age. *Psychology and Aging*, *15*, 417–436.

Linn, M. C., & Petersen, A. C. (1985). Emergence and characterization of sex differences in spatial ability: A meta-analysis. *Child Development*, *56*, 1479–1498.

Livingstone, M., & Hubel, D. (1988). Segregation of form, color, movement, and depth: Anatomy, physiology, and perception. *Science*, *240*, 740–749.

Logie, R. H. (1986). Visuo-spatial processing in working memory. *Quarterly Journal of Experimental Psychology*, *38A*, 229–247.

Logie, R. H. (1989). Characteristics of visual short-term memory. *European Journal of Cognitive Psychology*, *1*, 275–284.

Logie, R. H. (1990). Visuo-spatial short-term memory: Visual working memory or visual buffer? In C. Cornoldi & M. A. McDaniel (Eds.), *Imagery and cognition* (pp. 77–102). New York: Springer-Verlag.

Logie, R. H. (1995). *Visuo-spatial working memory*. Hove, UK: Lawrence Erlbaum Associates Ltd.

Logie, R. H., & Marchetti, C. (1991). Visuo-spatial working memory: Visual, spatial or central executive. In R. H. Logie & M. Denis (Eds.), *Mental images in human cognition* (pp. 105–115). Amsterdam: North-Holland, Elsevier.

Logie, R. H., & Pearson, D. (1997). The inner eye and the inner scribe of visuo-spatial working memory: Evidence from developmental fractioning. *European Journal of Cognitive Psychology*, *9*, 241–257.

Loomis, J. M., Klatzky, R. L., Golledge, R. G., Cicinelli, J. G., Pellegrino, J. W., & Fry, P. A. (1993). Nonvisual navigation by blind and sighted: Assessment of path integration ability. *Journal of Experimental Psychology: General*, *122*, 73–91.

Loring-Meier, S., & Halpern, D. F. (1999). Sex differences in visuospatial working memory: Components of cognitive processing. *Psychonomic Bulletin and Review*, *6*, 464–471.

Lummis, M., & Stevenson, H. W. (1990). Gender differences in beliefs and achievement: A cross-cultural study. *Developmental Psychology*, *26*, 254–263.

Lustig, C., May, C. P., & Hasher, L. (2001). Working memory span and the role of proactive interference. *Journal of Experimental Psychology: General*, *130*, 199–207.

Luzzatti, C., Vecchi, T., Agazzi, D., Cesa-Bianchi, M., & Vergani, C. (1998). A neurological dissociation between preserved visual and impaired spatial processing in mental imagery. *Cortex*, *34*, 461–469.

Lynn, R. (1994). Sex differences in intelligence and brain size: A paradox resolved. *Personality and Individual Differences*, *17*, 257–271.

Maccoby, E. E., & Jacklin, C. N. (1974). *The psychology of sex differences*. Stanford, CA: Stanford University Press.

MacDonald, M. C., & Christiansen, M. H. (2002). Reassessing working memory: Comment on Just and Carpenter (1992) and Waters and Caplan (1996). *Psychological Review*, *109*, 35–54.

Mammarella, N., Cornoldi, C., & Donadello, E. (in press). Visual but not spatial working memory deficit in children with spina bifida. *Brain and Cognition*.

Marinosson, G. L. (1974). Performance profile of normal, ESN, SSN (matched MA) on the revised ITPA. *Journal of Child Psychology and Psychiatry*, *5*, 139–148.

Marks, D. F. (1972). Individual differences in the vividness of visual imagery and their effect on function. In P. W. Sheehan (Ed.), *The function and nature of imagery* (pp. 83–108). New York: Academic Press.

Marmor, G. S. (1975). Development of kinetic images: When does the child first represent movement in mental images? *Cognitive Psychology*, *7*, 548–559.

Marmor, G. S. (1977). Mental rotation and number conservation: Are they related? *Developmental Psychology*, *13*, 320–325.

Marmor, G. S. (1978). Age at onset of blindness and the developmental of the semantics of colour names. *Journal of Experimental Child Psychology*, *25*, 267–278.

Marmor, G. S., & Zaback, L. A. (1976). Mental rotation by the blind: Does mental rotation depends on visual imagery? *Journal of Experimental Psychology: Human Perception and Performance*, *2*, 515–521.

Marr, D. (1982). *Vision*. San Francisco: Freeman & Company.

Marshall, J. C., & Newcombe, F. (1973). Patterns of paralexia: A psycholinguistic approach. *Journal of Psycholinguistic Research*, *2*, 175–199.

Marshall, S. P., & Smith, J. D. (1987). Sex differences in learning mathematics: A longitudinal study with item and error analyses. *Journal of Educational Psychology*, *79*, 372–383.

Martin, J. P., & Bell, J. (1943). A pedigree of mental defect showing X-linkage. *Journal of Neurology, Neurosurgery and Psychiatry*, *6*, 154–157.

Massironi, M., Rocchi, P., & Cornoldi, C. (2001). Does regularity affect the construction and memory of a mental image in the same way it affects a visual trace. *Psicologica*, *22*, 115–142.

Masunaga, H., & Horn, J. (2001). Expertise and age-related changes in components of intelligence. *Psychology and Aging*, *16*, 293–311.

Maylor, E. A., Vousdem, J. I., & Brown, G. D. A. (1999). Adult age differences in short-term memory for serial order: Data and a model. *Psychology and Aging*, *14*, 572–594.

Mayr, U., & Kliegl, R (1993). Sequential and coordinative complexity: Age-based processing limitations in figural transformations. *Journal of Experimental Psychology: Learning, Memory, and Cognition*, *19*, 1297–1320.

Mayr, U., Kliegl, R., & Krampe, R. T. (1996). Sequential and coordinative processing dynamics in figural transformations across the life span. *Cognition*, *59*, 61–90.

McConnell, J., & Quinn, J. G. (2000). Interference in visual working memory. *Quarterly Journal of Experimental Psychology*, *53A*, 53–67.

McDaniel, M. A., & Einstein, G. O. (1986). Bizarre imagery as an effective memory aid: The importance of distinctiveness. *Journal of Experimental Psychology: Learning, Memory and Cognition*, *12*, 54–65.

McDowd, J. M., & Shaw, R. (2000). Attention and aging: A functional perspective. In F. I. M. Craik & T. A. Salthouse (Eds.), *Handbook of aging and cognition* (2nd ed., pp. 221–292). Mahwah, NJ: Lawrence Erlbaum Associates Inc.

McGee, M. G. (1979). Human spatial abilities: Psychometric studies and environmental, genetic, hormonal, and neurological influences. *Psychological Bulletin*, *86*, 889–918.

McGlone, J. (1980). Sex differences in human brain asymmetry: Critical survey. *Behavioral and Brain Sciences*, *3*, 215–227.

McGuinness, D., Olson, A., & Chapman, J. (1990). Sex differences in incidental recall for words and pictures. *Learning and Individual Differences*, *2*, 263–285.

McKelvie, S. J. (1986). Effects of format of the vividness of visual imagery questionnaire on content validity, split-half reliability, and the role of memory in test-retest reliability. *British Journal of Psychology*, *77*, 229–236.

Melton, A. W. (1967). Repetition and retrieval from memory. *Science, 158*, 532.

Mendez, M. F. (2001). Visuospatial deficits with preserved reading ability in a patient with posterior cortical atrophy. *Cortex, 37*, 539–547.

Metzler, J., & Shepard, R. N. (1974). Transformational studies of the internal representation of three-dimensional objects. In R. L. Solso (Ed.), *Theories in cognitive psychology*. Potomac, MD: Lawrence Erlbaum Associates Inc.

Millar, S. (1994). *Understanding and representing space*. New York: Oxford University Press.

Milner, A. D., & Goodale, M. A. (1995). *The visual brain in action*. Oxford: Oxford University Press.

Milner, B. (1971). Interhemispheric differences in the localization of psychological processes in man. *British Medical Bulletin, 27*, 272–277.

Miyake, A. (2001). Individual differences in working memory: Introduction to the special section. *Journal of Experimental Psychology: General, 130*, 163–168.

Miyake, A., Friedman, N., Emerson, M. J., Witzki, A., & Howerter, A. (2000). The unity and diversity of executive functions and their contributions to complex "frontal lobe" tasks: A latent variable analysis. *Cognitive Psychology, 41*, 49–100.

Miyake, A., Friedman, N. P., Rettinger, D. A., Shah, P., & Hegarty, M. (2001). How are visuospatial working memory, executive functioning, and spatial abilities related? A latent-variable analysis. *Journal of Experimental Psychology: General, 130*, 621–640.

Miyake, A., & Shah, P. (Eds.) (1999). *Models of working memory*. Cambridge: Cambridge University Press.

Morris, R. G. (1996). Attentional and executive dysfunction. In R. G. Morris (Ed.), *The cognitive neuropsychology of Alzheimer-type dementia* (pp. 49–70). Oxford: Oxford University Press.

Morton, N., & Morris, R. G. (1995). Image transformation dissociated from visuospatial working memory. *Cognitive Neuropsychology, 12*, 767–791.

Mosedale, S. S. (1978). Science corrupted: Victorian biologists consider "the woman question". *Journal of the History of Biology, 11*, 1–55.

Munir, F., Cornish, K. M., & Wilding, J. (2000). Nature of the working memory deficit in fragile-X syndrome. *Brain and Cognition, 44*, 387–401.

Murphy, D., Allen, G., Haxby, J., Largay, K., Daly, E., White, B., Powell, C., & Shapiro, M. (1994). The effects of sex steroids, and the X chromosome, on female brain functions: A study of the neurosychology of adult Turner syndrome. *Neuropsychologia, 32*, 1309–1323.

Newcombe, N. (1982). Sex differences in spatial ability: Problems and gaps in current approaches. In M. Potegal (Ed.), *Spatial abilities development and physiological foundations*. New York: Academic Press.

Nichelli, F., Bulgheroni, S., & Riva., D. (2001). Developmental patterns of verbal and visuospatial spans. *Neurological Sciences, 22*, 377–384.

Nichelli, P. (1999). Visuospatial and imagery disorders. In G. Denes & L. Pizzamiglio (Eds.), *Handbook of clinical and experimental neuropsychology* (pp. 453–477). Hove, UK: Psychology Press.

Nichelli, P., & Venneri, A. (1995). Right hemisphere developmental learning disability: A case study. *Neurocase, 1*, 173–177.

O'Keefe, J., & Nadel, L. (1978). *The hippocampus as a cognitive map*. Oxford: Oxford University Press.

Oberauer, K., Sub, H. M., Schulze, R., Wilhelm, O., & Wittman, W. W. (2000). Working memory capacity: Facets of a cognitive construct. *Personality and Individual Differences, 29*, 1017–1045.

Oltman, P. K. (1968). A portable rod and frame test apparatus. *Perceptual and Motor Skills, 26*, 503–506.

Paivio, A. (1971). *Imagery and verbal processes*. New York: Holt, Reinhart & Winston.

Paivio, A., & Clark, J. M. (1991). Static versus dynamic imagery. In C. Cornoldi & M. A. McDaniel (Eds.), *Imagery and cognition* (pp. 221–245). New York: Springer-Verlag.

Paivio, A., & Harshman, R. A. (1983). Factor analysis of a questionnaire on imagery and verbal habits and skills. *Canadian Journal of Psychology*, *37*, 461–483.

Palladino, P., Cornoldi, C., De Beni, R., & Pazzaglia, F. (2001). Working memory and updating processes in reading comprehension. *Memory and Cognition*, *29*, 344–354.

Pani, J. R., Mervis, C. B., & Robinson, B. F. (1999). Global spatial organization by individuals with Williams syndrome. *Psychological Science*, *10*, 453–458.

Parkin, A.J., & Russo, R. (1990). Implicit and explicit memory and the automatic/effortful distinction. *European Journal of Cognitive Psychology*, *2*, 71–80.

Pascual-Leone, J. (1987). Organismic processes for neo-Piagetian theories: A dialectical causal account of cognitive development. *International Journal of Psychology*, *22*, 531–570.

Pascual-Leone, J., & Ijaz, H. (1989). Mental capacity testing as a form of intellectual-development assessment. In R. Samuda, S. Jong, J. Pascual-Leone, & J. Lewis. (Eds.), *Assessment and placement of minority students* (pp. 143–171). Toronto: Hogrefe.

Passolunghi, M. C., Cornoldi, C., & De Liberto, S. (1999). Working memory and intrusions of irrelevant information in a group of specific poor problem solvers. *Memory and Cognition*, *27*, 779–790.

Pazzaglia, F., & Cornoldi, C. (1999). The role of distinct components of visuo-spatial working memory in the processing of texts. *Memory*, *7*, 19–41.

Pearson, D., De Beni, R., & Cornoldi, C. (2001). The generation, maintenance, and transformation of visuo-spatial mental images. In M. Denis, R. H. Logie, C. Cornoldi, M. de Vega, & J. Engelkamp (Eds.), *Imagery, language and visuo-spatial thinking* (pp. 1–27). Hove, UK: Psychology Press.

Pezzini, G., Vicari, S., Volterra, V., Milani, L., & Ossella, M. T. (1999). Children with Williams syndrome: Is there a single neuropsychological profile? *Developmental Neuropsychology*, *15*, 141–155.

Phillips, W. A. & Christie, D. F. M. (1977). Components of visual memory. *Quarterly Journal of Experimental Psychology*, *29*, 117–133.

Piaget, J., & Inhelder, B. (1955). *De la logique de l'enfant à la logique de l'adolescent*. Paris: Presses Universitaire de France.

Piaget, J., & Inhelder, B. (1966). *L'image mentale chez l'enfant*. Paris: Presses Universitaire de France.

Pickering, S. J. (2001). Cognitive approaches to the fractionation of visuo-spatial working memory. *Cortex*, *37*, 457–473.

Pickering, S. J., Gathercole, S. E., Hall, M., & Lloyd, S. A. (2001). Development of memory for pattern and path: Further evidence for the fractionation of visual and spatial short-term memory. *Quarterly Journal of Experimental Psychology*, *54A*, 397–420.

Pickering, S. J., Gathercole, S. E., & Peaker, S. M. (1998). Verbal visuospatial short-term memory in children: Evidence for common and distinct mechanisms. *Memory and Cognition*, *26*, 1117–1130.

Poltrock, S. E., & Brown, P. (1984). Individual differences in visual imagery and spatial ability. *Intelligence*, *8*, 93–138.

Postma, A., & De Haan, E. H. F. (1996). What was there? Memory for object locations. *Quarterly Journal of Experimental Psychology*, *49A*, 178–199.

Postma, A., Izendoorn, R., & De Haan, E. H. F. (1998). Sex differences in object location memory. *Brain and Cognition*, *36*, 334–345.

Pylyshyn, Z. W. (1973). What the mind's eye tells the mind's brain: A critique of mental imagery. *Psychological Bulletin*, *80*, 1–24.

Quinn, J. G., & McConnell, J. (1996). Irrelevant pictures in visual working memory. *Quarterly Journal of Experimental Psychology*, *49A*, 200–215.

Quinn, J. G., & Ralston, G. E. (1986). Movement and attention in visual working memory. *Quarterly Journal of Experimental Psychology*, *38A*, 689–703.

Rabbitt, P. (1981). Cognitive psychology needs models for changes in performance with old age. In J. B. Long & A. D. Baddeley (Eds.), *Attention and performance IX* (pp. 555–573). Hillsdale, NJ: Lawrence Erlbaum Associates Inc.

Raz, N., Briggs, S. D., Marks, W., & Acker, J. D. (1999). Age-related deficits in generation and manipulation of mental images: II. The role of dorsolateral prefrontal cortex. *Psychology and Aging, 14*, 436–444.

Reiser, J. J., Guth, D. A., & Hill, E. W. (1986). Sensitivity to perspective structure while walking without vision. *Perception, 15*, 173–188.

Reiser, J. J., Hill, E., Talor, C., Bradfield, A., & Rosen, S. (1992). Visual experience, visual field size, and the development of nonvisual sensitivity to the spatial structure of outdoor neighborhoods explored by walking. *Journal of Experimental Psychology: General, 121*, 210–221.

Reiss, A. L., Freund, L. S., Baumgardner, T. L., Abrams, M. T., & Denckla, M. B. (1995). Contribution of the FMR-1 gene mutation to human intellectual dysfunction. *Nature Genetics, 11*, 331–334.

Rey, A. (1941). L'examen psychologique dans les cas d'encéphalophathie traumatique. *Archives de Psychologie, 28*, 286–340.

Reynolds, C. E., & Bigler, E. D. (1996). Factor structure, factor indexes, and other useful statistics for interpretation of the Test of Memory and Learning (TOMAL). *Archives of Clinical Neuropsychology, 11*, 29–43.

Richardson, J. T. E. (1991). Gender differences in imagery, cognition, and memory. In R. H. Logie & M. Denis (Eds.), *Mental images in human cognition* (pp. 271–303). Amsterdam: Elsevier.

Richardson, J. T. E. (1994). Gender differences in mental rotation. *Perceptual and Motor Skills, 78*, 435–448.

Richardson, J. T. E. (1996). Measures of effect size. *Behavior Research Methods, Instruments, & Computers, 28*, 12–22.

Richardson, J. T. E. (1997). Introduction to the study of gender differences in cognition. In P. J. Caplan, M. Crawford, J. S. Hyde, & J. T. E. Richardson, *Gender differences in human cognition* (pp. 3–29). New York: Oxford University Press.

Richardson, J. T. E. (2002). *The life and work of Howard Andrew Knox (1885–1949), the neglected pioneer of performance tests*. Manuscript in preparation.

Richardson, J. T. E., & Vecchi, T. (2002). A jigsaw-puzzle imagery task for assessing active visuospatial processes in old and young people. *Behavior Research Methods, Instruments & Computers, 34*, 69–82.

Rigoni, F., Gasparetto, R., & Cornoldi, C. (1999). Dissociazioni all'interno della memoria di Lavoro Visuospaziale: Evidenza di tre casi con disturbo non verbale dell'apprendimento. *Psichiatria dell'Infanzia e dell'Adolescenza, 66*, 205–216.

Roberts, R. J., & Aman, C. J. (1993). Developmental differences in giving directions: Spatial frames of reference and mental rotation. *Child Development, 64*, 1258–1270.

Rose, S. A., Feldman, J. F., & Jankowski, J. J. (2001). Visual short-term memory in the first year of life: Capacity and recency effects. *Developmental Psychology, 37*, 539–549.

Rourke, B. P. (1989). *Nonverbal disabilities, the syndrome and the model*. New York: Guilford Press.

Rovet, J. (1990). The cognitive and neuropsychological characteristics of children with Turner syndrome. In D. Berch & B. Bender (Eds.), *Sex chromosome abnormalities and human behavior: Psychological studies* (pp. 38–77). Boulder, CO: Westview.

Rovet, J. (1995). Turner syndrome, In B. P. Rourke (Ed.), *Syndrome of nonverbal learning disabilities* (pp. 351–371). New York: Guilford Press.

Rovet, J., & Netley, C. (1982). Processing deficits in Turner's syndrome. *Developmental Psychology, 18*, 77–94.

Rubini, V., & Cornoldi, C. (1985). Verbalizers and visualizers in child thinking and memory. *Journal of Mental Imagery, 9*, 77–90.

Saariluoma, P. (1994). Location coding in chess. *Quarterly Journal of Experimental Psychology*, *47A*, 607–630.

Saenger, P. (1996). Turner's syndrome. *New England Journal of Medicine*, *335*, 1749–1754.

Salthouse, T. A. (1991). *Theoretical perspectives on cognitive aging*. Hillsdale, NJ: Lawrence Erlbaum Associates Inc.

Salthouse, T. A. (1994). The nature of the influence of speed on adult age differences in cognition. *Developmental Psychology*, *30*, 240–259.

Salthouse, T. A. (1996). General and specific speed mediation of adult age differences in memory. *Journal of Gerontology: Psychological Sciences*, *51B*, 30–42.

Salthouse, T. A., Babcock, R. L., & Shaw, R. J. (1991). Effects of adult age on structural and operational capacities in working memory. *Psychology and Aging*, *6*, 118–127.

Salthouse, T. A., Babcock, R. L., Skovronek, E., Mitchell, D. R. D., & Palmon, R. (1990). Age and experience effects in spatial visualization. *Developmental Psychology*, *26*, 128–136.

Salthouse, T. A., & Coon, E. J. (1993). Influence of task-specific processing speed on age differences in memory. *Journal of Gerontology: Psychological Sciences*, *48*, 245–255.

Salthouse, T. A., & Meinz, V. E. (1995). Aging, inhibition, working memory, and speed. *Journal of Gerontology: Psychological Sciences*, *50*, 297–306.

Salthouse, T. A., & Mitchell, D. R. D. (1989). Structural and operational capacities in integrative spatial ability. *Psychology and Aging*, *4*, 18–25.

Salway, A. F. S., & Logie, R. H. (1995). Visuospatial working memory, movement control and executive demands. *British Journal of Psychology*, *86*, 253–269.

Schacter, D. L., & Tulving, E. (Eds.) (1994). *Memory systems 1994*. Cambridge, MA: MIT Press.

Schumann-Hengsteler, R. (1992). The development of visuo-spatial memory: How to remember location. *International Journal of Behavioral Development*, *15*, 455–471.

Schumann-Hengsteler, R. (1996). Visuospatial memory in children: Which memory codes are used in the concentration game? *Psychologische Beitraege*, *38*, 368–382.

Seigneuric, A., Ehrlich, M. F., Oakhill, J. V., & Yuill, N. M. (2000). Working memory resources and children's reading comprehension. *Reading and Writing*, *13*, 81–103.

Shah, P., & Miyake, A. (1996). The separability of working memory resources for spatial thinking and language processing: An individual differences approach. *Journal of Experimental Psychology: General*, *125*, 4–27.

Shallice, T. (1988). *From neuropsychology to mental structure*. Cambridge: Cambridge University Press.

Shapiro, M. B., Murphy, D. G. M., Hagerman, R. J., Azari, N. P., Alexander, G. E., Miezejeski, C. M., Hinton, V. J., Horwitz, B., Haxby, J. B., Kumar, A., White, B., & Grady, C. (1995). Adult fragile X syndrome: Neuropsychology, brain anatomy and metabolism. *American Journal of Medical Genetics*, *60*, 480–493.

Sharps, M. J., & Gollin, E. S. (1987). Speed and accuracy of mental image rotation in young and elderly adults. *Journal of Gerontology*, *42*, 342–344.

Sheehan, P. W. (1967). A shortened form of Betts' questionnaire upon mental imagery. *Journal of Clinical Psychology*, *23*, 386–389.

Shepard, R. N., & Metzler, J. (1971). Mental rotation of three-dimensional objects. *Science*, *171*, 701–703.

Sims, V. K., & Hegarty, M. (1997). Mental animation in the visuospatial sketchpad: Evidence from dual-task studies. *Memory and Cognition*, *25*, 321–332.

Smirnov, A. A. (1966). *Problemy psikhologii pamyati*. Moscow [Problems of the psychology of memory]. New York: Plenum Press (English edition published 1973).

Smith, E. E., & Jonides, J. (1999). Storage and executive processes in the frontal lobes. *Science*, *283*, 1657–1661.

Smyth, M. M., Pearson, N. A., & Pendleton, L. R. (1988). Movement and working memory: Patterns and positions in space. *Quarterly Journal of Experimental Psychology*, *40A*, 497–514.

Snodgrass, J. G., & Vanderwart, M. (1980). A standardized set of 260 pictures: Norms for Name Agreement, Image Agreement, Familiarity, and Visual Complexity. *Journal of Experimental Psychology: Human Learning and Memory, 6*, 174–215.

Sperling, G. (1960). The information available in brief visual presentations. *Psychological Monographs: General and Applied, 74*, 1–29.

Spreen, O., & Strauss, E. (1991). *A compendium of neuropsychological tests: Administration, norms, and commentary*. New York: Oxford University Press.

Stein, E. A., Rao, S. M., Bobholz, J. A., Fuller, S. A. Bloom, A. S., Cho, J. K., Pankewicz, J., & Harsch, H. (1995). Functional MRI of the human spatial memory. *Brain Mapping, Suppl. 1*, 328.

Stiles, J. (2000). Spatial cognitive development following prenatal or perinatal focal brain injury. In H. S. Levin & J. Grafman (Eds.), *Cerebral reorganization of function after brain damage* (pp. 201–217). New York: Oxford University Press.

Street, R. F. (1931). A Gestalt completion test. *Teachers College Contributions to Education, 481*.

Stuart, I. (1995). Spatial orientation and congenital blindness: A neuropsychological approach. *Journal of Visual Impairment and Blindness, 89*, 129–141.

Swanson, H. L. (1993). Individual differences in working memory: A model testing and subgroup analysis of learning-disabled and skilled readers. *Intelligence, 17*, 285–332.

Swanson, H. L. (1996). Individual and age related differences in children's working memory. *Memory and Cognition, 24*, 70–82.

Swanson, H. L., & Siegel, L. (2001). Learning disabilities as a working memory deficit. *Issues in Education, 7*, 1–48.

Taylor, A. K., Safanda, J. F., Fall, M. Z., Quince, C., Lang, K. A., Hull, C. E., Carpenter, I., Staley, L. W., & Hagerman, R. J. (1994). Molecular predictors of cognitive involvement in female carriers of fragile-X syndrome. *JAMA, 271*, 507–514.

Thinus-Blanc, C., & Gaunet, F. (1997). Representation of space in blind people: Vision as a spatial sense? *Psychological Bulletin, 121*, 20–42.

Thurstone, L. L. (1938). *Primary mental abilities. Psychometric monographs, 1*. Chicago: University of Chicago Press.

Thurstone, L. L., & Thurstone, T. G. (1947). *Primary mental abilities*. New York: Psychological Corporation.

Tinti, C., Cornoldi, C., & Marschark, M. (1997). Modality-specific auditory imaging and the interactive imagery effect. *European Journal of Cognitive Psychology, 9*, 417–436.

Tinti, C., Galati, D., Vecchio, M. G., De Beni, R., & Cornoldi, C. (1999). Interactive auditory and visual images in persons who are totally blind. *Journal of Visual Impairment and Blindness, 93*, 579–583.

Tressoldi, P. E. & Cornoldi, C. (2000). *Non-verbal profiles in mild mental retardation*. Paper presented at the third European conference "Psychological theory and research on mental retardation", Geneva, Switzerland, August 31–September 2.

Trojano, L., Grossi, D., Linden, D. E. J., Formisano, E., Goebel, R., Cirillo, S., Elefante, R., & Di Salle, F. (2002). Coordinate and categorical judgements in spatial imagery: An fMRI study. *Neuropsychologia, 40*, 1666–1674.

Turner, H. H. (1938). A syndrome of infantilism, congenital webbed neck and cubitus valgus. *Endocrinology, 23*, 566–578.

Tversky, B. (1969). Pictorial and verbal encoding in a short-term memory task. *Perception and Psychophysics, 6*, 225–233.

Tversky, B. (1974). Retrieval of pictorial and verbal stimulus codes. *Bulletin of the Psychonomic Society, 4*, 65–68.

Udwin, O., & Yule, W. (1991). A cognitive and behavioural phenotype in Williams syndrome. *Journal of Clinical and Experimental Neuropsychology, 13*, 232–244.

Uecker, A., Mangan, P. A., Obrzut, J. E., & Nadel, L. (1993). Down syndrome in neurobiological perspective: An emphasis on spatial cognition. *Journal of Clinical Child Psychology*, *22*, 266–276.

Uecker, A., Obrzut, J. E., & Nadel, L. (1994). Mental rotation performance by learning disabled and Down's syndrome children: A study of imaginal development. *Developmental Neuropsychology*, *10*, 395–411.

Ungerleider, L. G., & Haxby, J. V. (1994). "What" and "where" in the human brain. *Current Opinion Neurobiology*, *4*, 157–165.

Ungerleider, L. G., & Mishkin, M. (1982). Two cortical visual systems. In D. J. Ingle, M. S. Goodale, & R. J. W. Mansfield (Eds.), *The analysis of visual behavior* (pp. 549–586). Cambridge, MA: MIT Press.

Vandenberg, S. G., & Kuse, A. R. (1978). Mental rotations, a group test of three-dimensional spatial visualization. *Perceptual and Motor Skills*, *47*, 599–604.

Vecchi, T. (1998). Visuo-spatial limitations in congenitally totally blind people. *Memory*, *6*, 91–102.

Vecchi, T. (2001). Visuo-spatial processing in congenitally blind people: Is there a gender-related preference? *Personality and Individual Differences*, *29*, 1361–1370.

Vecchi, T., & Cornoldi, C. (1999). Passive storage and active manipulation in visuo-spatial working memory: Further evidence from the study of age differences. *European Journal of Cognitive Psychology*, *11*, 391–406.

Vecchi, T., & Girelli, L. (1998). Gender differences in visuo-spatial processing: The importance of distinguishing between passive storage and active manipulation. *Acta Psychologica*, *99*, 1–16.

Vecchi, T., Monticelli, M. L., & Cornoldi, C. (1995) Visuo-spatial working memory: Structures and variables affecting a capacity measure. *Neuropsychologia*, *33*, 1549–1564.

Vecchi, T., Phillips, L. H., & Cornoldi, C. (2001). Individual differences in visuo-spatial working memory. In M. Denis, R. H. Logie, C. Cornoldi, M. de Vega, & J. Engelkamp (Eds.), *Imagery, language and visuo-spatial thinking* (pp. 29–58). Hove, UK: Psychology Press.

Vecchi, T., & Richardson, J. T. E. (2000). Active processing in visuo-spatial working memory. *Cahiers de Psychologie Cognitive*, *19*, 3–32.

Vecchi, T., & Richardson, J. T. E. (2001). Measures of visuospatial short-term memory: The Knox cube imitation test and the Corsi blocks test compared. *Brain and Cognition*, *46*, 291–295.

Vecchi, T., Richardson, J. T. E., & Cavallini, E. (2002). *Processing and complexity effects in working memory*. Manuscript submitted for publication.

Vecchi, T., Saveriano, V., & Paciaroni, L. (1998/1999). Storage and processing working memory functions in Alzheimer-type dementia. *Behavioural Neurology*, *11*, 227–231.

Vecchio, L. (1991). *La memoria di lavoro: Studio sperimentale sulla componente visuo-spaziale* [Working memory: An experimental study of the visuo-spatial component]. Doctoral thesis, University of Pavia, Italy.

Vederhus, L., & Krekling, S. (1996). Sex difference in visual spatial ability in 9-year-old children. *Intelligence*, *23*, 33–43.

Verhaeghen, P., & De Meersman, L. (1998). Aging and the Stroop effect: A meta-analysis. *Psychology and Aging*, *13*, 120–126.

Vicari, S., Albertini, G., & Caltagirone, C. (1992). Cognitive profiles in adolescents with mental retardation. *Journal of Intellectual Disability Research*, *36*, 415–423.

Vicari, S., Bellucci, S., & Carlesimo, G. A. (2000b). Implicit and explicit memory: A functional dissociation in persons with Down syndrome. *Neuropsychologia*, *38*, 240–251.

Vicari, S., Bellucci, S., & Carlesimo, G. A. (in press). Visual and spatial working memory dissociation: Evidence from a genetic syndrome. *Developmental Medicine and Child Neurology*.

Vicari, S., Brizzolara, D., Carlesimo, G. A., Pezzini, G., & Volterra, V. (1996b). Memory abiliites in children with Williams syndrome. *Cortex*, *32*, 503–514.

Vicari, S., Carlesimo, G., Brizzolara, D., & Pezzini, G. (1996a). Short-term memory in children with Williams syndrome: A reduced contribution of lexical–semantic knowledge to word span. *Neuropsychologia*, *34*, 919–925.

Vicari, S., Carlesimo, A., & Caltagirone, C. (1995). Short-term memory in persons with intellectual disabilities and Down's syndrome. *Journal of Intellectual Disability Research*, *39*, 532–537.

Vicari, S., Caselli, M. C., & Tonucci, F. (2000a). Asynchrony of lexical and morphosyntactic development in children with Down syndrome. *Neuropsychologia*, *38*, 634–644.

Vicari, S., Nocentini, U., & Caltagirone, C. (1994). Neuropsychological diagnosis of aging in adults with Down syndrome. *Developmental Brain Dysfunction*, *7*, 340–348.

Vogel, J. M. (1980). Limitations on children's short-term memory for left–right orientation. *Journal of Experimental Child Psychology*, *19*, 3–32.

Volterra, V., Longobardi, E., Pezzini, G., Vicari, S., & Antenore, C. (1999). Visuo-spatial and linguistic abilities in a twin with Williams syndrome. *Journal of Intellectual Disability Research*, *43*, 294–305.

Voyer, D., Voyer, S., & Bryden, M. P. (1995). Magnitude of sex differences in spatial abilities: A meta-analysis and consideration of critical variables. *Psychological Bulletin*, *117*, 250–270.

Walker, A. (1850). *Woman physiologically considered*. New York: Langley.

Walker, P., Hitch, G. J., Dewhurst, S. A., Whiteley, H. E., & Brandimonte, M. A. (1997). The representation of nonstructural information in visual memory: Evidence from image combination. *Memory and Cognition*, *25*, 484–490.

Wang, P. P., & Bellugi, U. (1994). Evidence from two genetic syndromes for a dissociation between verbal and visuo-spatial short-term memory. *Journal of Clinical and Experimental Neuropsychology*, *16*, 317–322.

Wang, P. P., Doherty, S., Rourke, S. B., & Bellugi, U. (1995). Unique profile of visuo-perceptual skills in a genetic syndrome. *Brain and Cognition*, *29*, 54–65.

Waters, G. S., & Caplan, D. (1996). The capacity theory of sentence comprehension: Critique of Just and Carpenter (1992). *Psychological Review*, *103*, 761–772.

Wechsler, D. (1944). *The measurement of adult intelligence* (3rd ed.). Baltimore, MD: Williams & Wilkins.

Wechsler, D. (1945). A standardized memory scale for clinical use. *Journal of Psychology*, *19*, 87–95.

Wechsler, D. (1949). *Manual for the Wechsler Intelligence Scale for Children*. New York: Psychological Corporation.

Wechsler, D. (1981). *Wechsler Adult Intelligence Scale–Revised*. New York: Psychological Corporation.

Welford, A. T. (1958). *Ageing and human skill*. London: Oxford University Press.

Williams, J. C. P., Barratt-Boyes, B. G., & Lowe, J. B. (1961). Supravalvular aortic stenosis. *Circulation*, *24*, 1311–1318.

Witkin, M. A., Oltman, P. K., Raskin, E. & Karp, S. A. (1971). *A manual for the Embedded Figures test*. Palo Alto, CA: Consulting Psychologists Press.

Wynn, T. (1989). *The evolution of spatial competence*. Chicago: University of Illinois Press.

Yee, P. L., Hunt, E., & Pellegrino, J. W. (1991). Coordinating cognitive information: Task effects and individual differences in integrating information from several sources. *Cognitive Psychology*, *23*, 615–680.

Zimler, J., & Keenan, J. M. (1983). Imagery in the congenitally blind: How visual are visual images? *Journal of Experimental Psychology: Learning, Memory and Cognition*, *9*, 269–282.

Author index

Subject index